Woman
By God's Design

Cynthia McGill

ISBN 979-8-88943-764-2 (paperback)
ISBN 979-8-88943-765-9 (digital)

Christian Faith Publishing
832 Park Avenue
Meadville, PA 16335
www.christianfaithpublishing.com

Printed in the United States of America

Contents

Introduction

There are many facets of every woman, and we all have been uniquely designed and fashioned as it pleased God. When I reflect on my life, I have come to realize just how valuable we are as women, and I wrote this book to highlight some of the women patriarchs of scripture, showcase their strengths, and identify their struggles. Every woman, regardless of where she may be on the spectrum of life, will appreciate the similarities that we all share. Although we make up a diverse group of ethnicities, with different backgrounds, experiences, and interests, we share the one common denominator: we are women! I believe that each of us will make an impact with our contributions, accomplishments, and successes, no matter how great or small they may be!

We are multidimensional because of our many abilities, gifts, and talents. A woman by God's design is not one who can be summed up and tucked away in a small canister! Oh no, she is too big to be captured as one-dimensional. She exemplifies the glory of God, and His goodness is demonstrated in her life.

She is called to serve in many capacities, and she does so with a spirit of excellence!

My hope is that as you read this book, you will be inspired, informed, encouraged, and even excited that you are a woman! It is my prayer that your heart will be open to appreciate the strengths and the struggles that we all share alike, and at the same time, we can celebrate our individuality, for each of us is a woman by God's design!

CHAPTER 1

The Woman as God Intended—His Plan

Every woman is created by God and for His intended purpose. He has preordained a blueprint of our lives before we were even formed in our mother's womb. God, our Creator, *knew* us before we were even conceived! In His infinite wisdom, He perfectly outlined and sketched the blueprint of our lives. We were strategically designed for a specific purpose with a specified window of time to exist on this planet. Our Creator fashioned us with all the distinct physical characteristics as He desired to do so.

Our assignment and purpose lie dormant inside each of us. And when we awaken to Him, we *discover* who we are and what our assignment and purpose in this life will be.

I knew you before I formed you in your mother's womb.

Before you were born, I set you apart and
appointed you as my prophet to the nations.
(Jer. 1:5)

Let us consider here exactly what God's intention was. He had already decided what Jeremiah would do on earth. He had already given him the assignment of becoming a prophet to the nations. God is a purposeful Being. Everything that He created was planned and serves a specific purpose.

And so it is with the woman. God created women in a special and unique way. We are a spirit, we possess a soul, and we live in a body. We are wives, mothers, sisters, friends, colleagues, coworkers, nieces, aunts, grandmothers, educators, mayors, governors, administrators, pastors. Yes, we operate in many functions, and we do them all well!

As we submit our lives to God and draw closer to Him, our purpose becomes clear and more precise. It is then that we begin to realize the predetermined plan of God for our lives.

We now begin to recognize that we are a creation of God. And because He is the Creator, He is the only one who can reveal to us *who* and *what* His purpose is for our lives.

When God created woman, it was His intention that she would be created in His image and His likeness.

So, God created man in his own image.
In the image of God, he created them; male
and female he created them. (Gen. 1:27)

When we consider the definition of what it means to create, we will find that it is the action or process of bringing something new into existence or formation, to design. When God created us in His image, that does not mean that God Himself is in human form; rather it means that humans were created to be equivalent to God in our morals, our intellect, and in spirit, for God is a spirit.

We know that the creation of the first man and woman were in His image and His likeness, which would make them spiritual beings as well. The man and woman were designed to function from a higher and more elevated platform in life than any of God's other creations. This would also make them the only form of creation capable of giving praise and worship to God.

We know that God is a spirit, "for God is Spirit, so those who worship him must worship in spirit and in truth" (John 4:24).

The first man, Adam, was formed from the dust of the earth, giving him a physical structure. So that which was created as spirit and formed from dust is now housed or contained in that which is physical—a body.

Although man was the last of the creation of God, created on the sixth day, man was the most excellent of all creation because he was made in God's image! To be made in God's image would mean that we were created as a representation of God Himself. We were created to express the attributes and the external resemblance of God, our Creator.

God breathed into the nostrils of man in creation, and the man became a living person.

> Then the Lord God formed the man
> from the dust of the ground. He breathed the
> breath of life into the man's nostrils, and the
> man became a living person. (Gen. 2:7)

God then decided that it was not good for the man to be alone, so He formed the first woman, Eve. I have always found this intriguing that our Creator only had one option in mind for the man, and that was the woman. God, in His infinite wisdom, could have created another beast or an additional bird or even perhaps a few more creatures. But instead He wanted to pair the man with the woman! God's purpose for Eve was to be a helper for the first man, Adam. Often, when we hear the word *helper,* we think of it in a condescending way. We think of a helper as being less than or subservient to the other who is receiving the help. But this is not how God thought of the woman! God thought of us as equal created beings to the man. In fact, the woman would be the physical embodiment of God's help for the man. She would be the one that would bring balance to him and the counterpart that would be *suitable and complementary* for Adam. When we consider the meaning of *suitable* in this context, it reveals that God created Eve to be equal to Adam, opposite of Adam, and very capable of helping

Adam. She would be his companion, who would speak up and advise.

She would also be the one by his side to face the joys and the sorrows of life together. She was not to be considered as less than, for they both had a mind to think, a heart to feel, and a spirit that would live forever. Eve, the woman, would be formed *from* the man and *for* the man. Both the man and the woman were created to be unique with different gifts and talents and yet equal and fitting companions to one another.

This woman, by God's design, was taken from a rib, out of the man's side, while he slept. God caused a deep sleep upon the man so that he would not experience any pain or grief from the forming of his counterpart that God was providing for him.

She was not taken out of his head to rule over him, neither was she taken out from his feet to be trampled on by him. Instead, she was taken from his side to accompany him and give him companionship, and yet she would be equal to him. This woman would have the corresponding quality as the man and the equivalence of him.

It was God's intent that the man and the woman would reign in life together as one flesh.

> This explains why a man leaves his father
> and mother and is joined to his wife, and the
> two are united into one. (Gen. 2:24)

Another scripture is found in Proverbs 18:22.

> The man who finds a wife finds a treasure, and he receives favor from the Lord.

Eve, the first woman, was created by God's design—a spiritual being, possessing a soul, and living in a physical body.

She was created to be a woman (man with a womb).

God designed this woman in such a unique way that she would be the only creation to possess the physical anatomy enabling her to conceive, incubate, and give birth to another human being that would be a part of her, her husband, and a living spirit as God the Creator!

So it is with the woman who was taken out from the man. She is now alive to her purpose and her passion because the breath of God has awakened her!

Eve would be the first and only woman not born of a woman but formed from a man.

> So the Lord God caused the man to fall into a deep sleep. While the man slept, the Lord God took out one of the man's ribs and closed the opening. Then the Lord God made a woman from the rib, and he brought her to the man. (Gen. 2:21–22)

When God completed His forming of the beautiful woman, He presented her to the man.

God, the Heavenly Father, presented His first daughter to her husband in the same way that an earthly father would present his daughter in marriage. What a beautiful wedding this had to be! God had joined them together as one, perfect and in complete *harmony with Him and with each other.*

The man declared in Genesis 2:23, "This is now bone of my bone, and flesh of my flesh." The man recognized that Eve, his wife, was a part of him, and she would be all that he would need to reign in life.

It was Adam who called her "woman" or "womb-man." And now, presenting Mr. and Mrs. Adam and Eve!

The first man and woman! God had set them up to live in a perfect garden, a paradise, abundantly supplied with everything that they would ever need.

It was not God's intent or part of His plan that the man and woman would be acquainted with lack, poverty, sin, or death. God, who is rich in supply, had now provided His riches to the first man and the first woman. God's heart for them was to live in perfect peace and be abundantly supplied.

They were rich in provision, for God the Creator had supplied them with plant life and all the fruits and vegetation from the earth. He also provided streams of water to refresh and revive the garden of Eden.

They had also been given the authority to reign and to rule in life.

Then God blessed them and said, "Be fruitful and multiply. Fill the earth and govern it. Reign over the fish in the sea, the birds in the sky, and all the animals that scurry along the ground." (Gen. 1:28)

Every wild animal and bird that God created, He bought to Adam so that he could choose the name for each one, And whatever Adam called that creature, that became the name! This demonstrated the authority that the man had received from God!

Adam had now executed the perfect plan of God and the authority given unto him when he named the creatures. His authority remained intact and held power.

This was God's original plan, that man would have dominion, power, and authority in the earth as God had in the heavens.

God had already given the man his instructions.

But the LORD God commanded him, "You may freely eat the fruit of every tree in the garden except the tree of the knowledge of good and evil. If you eat its fruit, you are sure to die." (Gen. 2:16–17)

The man and his wife could freely eat and enjoy every tree in the garden, but they were instructed not to eat of the tree of the recognition or knowledge of good and evil. God had told them that if they did eat of this tree, they would surely die! His instructions were precise and clear. Everything that God had created was GOOD. There was no flaw or error in all of creation. The man and woman were granted access to every part of the garden and all that it offered.

The man was given the responsibility to attend and watch over the garden. God had given them total dominion and authority to operate and reign over all that He, the Creator, had made. He did not leave them in need of anything, and all that was required of them was to abstain from the *one* thing, the *one* tree, the tree of recognition of what was good and what was evil.

CHAPTER 2

The Woman's Greatest Enemy—Deception

As a woman by God's design, it is important that we listen and obey the voice of our Heavenly Father. We must recognize that He is our Creator, and we are His creation. When He speaks to us and gives us instruction, we can't afford to take His command lightly, because every instruction is linked to an event in our future! If we do not obey His instruction, we open ourselves up to deception.

Deception is defined as the act of causing someone to accept as true or valid, what is false or invalid. It also is being deceitful, misleading, and deluding someone with trickery.

In Genesis 3:1, it states, "The serpent was the shrewdest of all the wild animals the Lord God had made." He was sharp-witted and very astute. In the original plan of God, the serpent was an angel of light and an attendant upon God's throne. But because of rebellion against God's crown and dignity, the serpent no longer wanted to worship and praise God the Creator; instead, he desired to be praised himself and started a revolution to defy God the Creator!

He no longer wanted to be a part of God's creation, but instead he wanted the position of Creator and have influence over creation. He wanted to be lifted high and required the worship for himself.

The serpent came with one objective: to deceive the woman. He knew that in order to get his devious plan in motion, he would need to defy God. And to do that, he would target God's highest creation!—yes, mankind, the only creation of God that had the ability to fellowship with God and worship God.

The serpent also knew that Eve, the woman, was designed by God to conceive, incubate, and eventually give birth to the seed of Adam. He understood her role in the reproduction of human beings on the earth.

So what better way to sabotage the plan of God for procreation? By deceiving the first woman, the mother of all living, who would ultimately be the portal by which all of mankind would be born!

Let's examine how this plot unfolded. First, the serpent knew that Adam was the one who had received the instructions regarding the tree of the recognition of good and evil.

He also was aware that if he could engage the woman into a conversation, that would allow him the opportunity to determine if the woman knew about the instructions and if she would obey those instructions.

As women, it is vital that we realize that when we engage in conversation with anyone, the words that they speak are being deposited into our mind and ultimately into our heart. It is important to understand that women are receivers! Take a moment to consider the physical anatomy of the woman. There is a specific part of the female body that is designed to complement a specific part of the male. When those parts make contact, the male will function as the giver, and the female functions as the receiver.

This is also true of us, as women, when we hear words. We are receiving those words! These words will create imagery and mental images. Words are very powerful, and they will influence us, even when they are spoken from an unreliable source. Once those words have been deposited inside of us, they begin to sprout and grow. The serpent knew that his conversation with Eve would create doubt and suspicion in the mind of the woman about what God had said. Satan's word would cause her to rethink *the Word* that God had said.

The serpent would position himself in order to distract Eve, to take advantage of her in an unsuspecting moment. He engaged the woman in conversation by asking her a question, although he knew that the man was the one to whom God had given the command. So to begin with, the serpent was working against the divine order of God. God had given Adam the instructions, so why did the serpent ask the woman when he could have asked the man? Secondly, he caused Eve to reconsider what the command of God had been. When the serpent was questioning Eve, he focused on what God had *restricted from them*. And yet when God gave the command to Adam, God's focus was on what he had *freely given to them*. In Genesis 2:16, it states, "And the Lord God commanded the man, saying, of every tree of the garden you may freely eat..." This shows us that God intended for man to have abundance. He wanted them to enjoy all the trees in the garden. There were plenty of trees that they could freely eat of and enjoy. They would have more than enough.

In Genesis 3:1, it states, "...and he (the serpent) said to the woman, Has God indeed said, you shall not eat of every tree of the garden?"

This shows us that the serpent wanted the woman to focus on restrictions. He wanted her to think that perhaps God was withholding something from them.

Adam, her husband, was with her; however, the conversation was totally between the serpent and the woman. Adam did not have any dialogue with the serpent. Eve was the one engaging in this conversation with the serpent. The two of them had a back-and-forth exchange of words, and the man, Adam, never engaged in the dialogue. Yes, Adam was physically present, but in this moment, Eve was the only one responding to the serpent. Adam had declared that the two would be one flesh. He had already said that she was flesh of his flesh and bone of his bone. What was going on here? Why did Adam say nothing? I believe this is a question that has been raised countless times, and there are several views on the subject. However, I wish to take another approach and focus on the woman.

He began a conversation with Eve by asking her a question.

> "Did God really say you must not eat the fruit from any of the trees in the garden?"
>
> "Of course, we may eat fruit from the trees in the garden," the woman replied.
>
> "It's only the fruit from the tree in the middle of the garden that we are not allowed to eat. God said, 'You must not eat it or even touch it; if you do, you will die.'" (Gen. 3:1–3)

The woman knew what God had said. In her response, she told the deceiver exactly what the instructions had been. Now take a moment to consider this: The serpent knew exactly what God had said also!

It is evident in his question: "Did God really say you must not eat the fruit from any of the trees in the garden?"

Think about this: If he had no idea of the instructions that God had already given to them, his question would have been more open-ended, like "What did God say?"

The serpent presented the question to the woman to make her entertain doubt about *exactly* what God had said. This is seen in her response when she said that they could not touch the fruit. The truth is, God never mentioned anything about not touching the fruit; however, it is important to point out that in order to eat of the tree, they would need to touch the fruit. It is clear to see that as Eve entertained the conversation with the serpent, she herself was becoming somewhat unsettled. This is what Satan does to all of us when we continue to listen to his words, instead of obeying what God has spoken. The serpent sowed doubt in Eve's mind about what God had said. This demonstrates his denial of the truth of God's Word, God's character, and God's motives.

As the conversation continued with the doubt and denial, this produced disobedience in the heart of the woman. And there it was! The serpent had now deceived Eve by being manipulative. Her heart was now involved. Her desire had now changed as she was being influenced by the trickery of the serpent. Now she began to look at the fruit of the tree, and she *saw* that it was indeed a beautiful tree. She also began to desire the fruit and then shared with her husband, Adam, who was with her!

> The woman was convinced. She saw that the tree was beautiful, and its fruit looked delicious, and she wanted the wisdom it would give her, so she took some of the fruit and ate it. Then she gave some to her husband, who was with her, and he ate it, too. (Gen. 3:6)

It is now clear to me what took place on this day. Satan had deceived the woman. He had manipulated the situation and stimulated the senses of the woman. Her sense of sight, desire, and touch had all been aroused. The woman saw with her eyes. She then had desire in her heart, and finally she touched the fruit and ate of it. Not only had she been deceived, but she would also now influence her husband. He participated willingly because he was now influenced by his wife.

The power of influence is very significant. And although this is not the way we want to use it, this situation clearly demonstrates the affect that we, as women, can have because of our influence.

Let us be reminded that the serpent was an astute, crafty, and subtle creature. He already knew the demeanor of the woman. He probably had observed her over a period in the garden and had realized that she was not only a beautiful creation of God, but she was also a creature of influence. The serpent wanted to interject influence. This is the one thing that he craved the most and still desires even today. The serpent set his sights on Eve because she was a woman of influence. We must realize that a person with influence has a certain amount of control and power. One who has influence can affect or change people or situations in an indirect but important way. An individual with influence has an element of persuasion on them. This can be positive or negative, depending upon the individual's own beliefs. We fail to see that the enemy will always target the one who is most likely to have influence because that one's downfall will not only impact them, but it will impact many others as well.

We must understand that this is the nature of Satan, the tempter. He always makes suggestions, which will cause us to question our own beliefs, lean to our own understanding, and many times rely on a soulish emotion as a response.

Satan understood one thing about the woman that we sometimes don't even realize about ourselves, and that is how *influential* we really are. Yes, we are invaluable and precious, and there is no price that can be assigned to our worth. And one of the greatest effects that we have is influence!

Therefore, it is so vital for us to know the Word of God and to receive His Word! When the Word of God is in our heart, it will set up the standard for our life. This will keep us from going back and forth because we know what God has said. His Word will be our light and our lamp. We will not be double-minded when we know what God has said in His Word. We will not find ourselves wavering between what we must do or what not to do when we have His word in our heart. We will then be able to recognize deception when it approaches us. The spirit of deception is very subtle. It presents itself as genuine and true but in fact is cunning and full of trickery. It does not want to be discovered or seen; however, it cannot hide behind the truth. When the truth of God's Word is revealed, that light will shine on all darkness and deception to expose it.

It is also necessary to mention that Eve was just fine with the plan of God until she was enticed to consider another option. Many times, as women, we may know the will of God for our lives in a specific area, but Satan has a way of presenting things to us so that we *feel* we have missed out on something better. His mission is to lead us away from the plan of God by appealing to our emotional makeup. He stirs up the desires and cravings within our soul and appeases us with what we see, hear, feel, and touch. He has a clever way of suggesting to us another option, an alternative, another way.

Consider this scripture in 1 John 2:16, which reads, "For everything in the world—the lust of the flesh, the lust of the eyes, and the pride of life, comes not from the Father but from the world."

Let's consider this practical example: You are believing God for a certain position of advancement in your career. You have prayed diligently about it, and God presents an opportunity. You feel very certain about this position, interview for it, and then wait for a follow-up call from the hiring manager. Meanwhile, during the wait, you now hear about another opportunity for advancement, and you become distracted by it since the company has posted the position with a higher salary. However, after doing your research, you learn that the benefits are not as good as the position that you already interviewed for. You also come to realize that this position will cause you to be away from your family for more than ten hours each day, several days per week. This will cause you to miss important events and family time. Sound familiar? We must be very prayerful in these moments because once you have settled in your heart what you know God is giving to you, it is then that something else will present itself to distract and confuse you. We must realize that our enemy, the devil, can sabotage your goal by giving you another goal! Stay in peace with what God has already spoken in your heart, and do not allow the trickster to deceive you. We must remember that whatever captures our attention will distract us from our goal.

There are several views on what took place in the perfect garden of Eden on that fateful day. But if we could collect every viewpoint, every perspective, and theological theory, the sum of it all would be that on that day mankind (Adam/Eve) decided that they were strong enough and wise enough to live independently from God, their Creator! That decision thrust the entire human race into jeopardy. Now every person born into this world has their own will and desire to live independently of what God's will and desire is for their lives!

Each of us fell into this state of mind as a result of their decision, but thanks be unto God, who has delivered us from this never-ending cycle through Jesus Christ!

As Christian women, it is so important that we guard access to ourselves. We can't allow just anyone into our space and into our lives. Every person that we grant access should qualify to be in that place and is sent by God. I am not suggesting that you live in a state of isolation or fear of people; however, it is important that we recognize what the motive and purpose is for everyone that we allow into our lives. It is a fact that when God wants to bless us, He may send a person into our life. At the same time, when Satan wants to distract us, He also may send a person into our life. We must be wise to know the difference!

We must set some restrictions in our lives and be very selective about who may enter the portal. This will guarantee that our lives will not be interrupted by any satanic or demonic forces. In 2 Corinthians 4:4, Satan is known as the "god of this world" or "god of this age" because of the influence that he has on those who still have not believed. As women of faith, we must realize this truth: Satan does have a certain amount of authority in the earth realm. This is because, when God gave man authority in the beginning, man was deceived and was tricked out of the authority, giving it to the devil!

Because of this, he can operate in the lives of unbelievers, as well as Christians who are not walking by the leading of the spirit of God! He can influence them in their opinions, philosophies, hopes, and goals in such a way that they are under his control without even realizing it! Everything that he presents to us is full of darkness, lies, and deception! It is his goal to keep us blinded of his schemes, his plots, and his strategies. When we fail to recognize that he is behind all the trickery, we will begin to operate under the influence of his power. He is the one behind false beliefs in this world, which keeps us constantly in search of the truth.

Everything that Satan does is orchestrated to make us believe that we are self-sufficient and totally independent of God! He himself already knows that God is sovereign and that God is the Creator of this universe; however, he constantly imprisons us in our minds and keeps us in a never-ending cycle of self-gratification and disobedience to God. He has greatly deceived us into thinking that freedom is doing what we want!

His desire is to mislead us and have us believe that we don't have to answer or be accountable to anyone but ourselves.

He continues to veil the truth from us, which is that true freedom comes without penalty when we obey God! God's desire is that we enjoy all that He has given to us without restraint or restrictions.

Satan wants us to lose our moral consciousness and devalue ourselves, as well as others. He does not want us to recognize God as our Creator and subsequently identify ourselves as creations of God, made in His image and likeness. Instead, our adversary wants us to constantly be in pursuit of greatness that seemingly comes from outside of us, rather than realizing that because of Christ, the greater One is on the inside of us! If we are tricked and operate from this inferior platform, we will never reach the optimal level that God intended for us in the beginning. We become Satan's puppets, performing on his demand because we fail to acknowledge God and to establish a relationship with Him. We fail to accept His gift to us, which is Jesus! We continue to force ourselves to live this life in our own strength and never tap into the strength of God! We continue to limit ourselves because we ourselves are limited! We do this rather than submitting ourselves completely to God so that *He* can elevate us. This is the plot of Satan: to keep us in a confined space by deceiving us!

God's highest desire for us as His creation, His woman, was to live at the most excellent level, a level in which boundaries would not be familiar, for He wanted us to experience all that He had created, all of who He is, and all that we are in Him. It was His desire that we would be submitted to Him and allow Him to manifest all His goodness in us and through us. It was His intent to set us above and not beneath. He desired that we would always be the head and never the tail. God's plan for us was perfect in every way!

God demonstrated this principle Himself in His perfect creation of man, woman, and even the garden of Eden. Yes, all His creation was perfect, and yet God had set up boundaries.

He teaches us something right there and that is, *perfection remains intact because of boundaries*! Where there are no boundaries, there is no accountability, and eventually, ruin and destruction will enter in!

Man is the highest form of creation and the only creation made in the image and likeness of God. Man is the only creation that has this power—the power to make a choice, the power to choose what we desire, and to disregard what we wish to reject.

Satan's plot would be to deceive the woman, and she in turn would influence her husband!

> And when the woman saw that the tree was good for food, and that it was pleasant to the eyes, and a tree to be *desired to make one wise, she took of the fruit thereof, and did eat, and gave also unto her husband with her; and he did eat.* (Gen. 3:6)

The scripture clearly states that her husband (Adam) was with her, and he did eat.

Both the man and woman knew what God's instructions had been. However, because the serpent's plot was very thought out and well planned, he was certain that he could *deceive* the woman, and the woman would *influence* the man.

I believe that Adam loved his wife, and the serpent knew this. He also knew that the woman was the *visible glory* of the man. Because of that, Eve would have great influence on her husband; after all, she was *his visible glory.* Yes, it is true that we, as women, have influence, but that influence should be under the influence of the Holy Spirit!

He also knew that Eve, the woman, would become the mother of all living, the first woman, the door to all mankind, and so the serpent started the conversation filled with vile and deceit! The serpent was not only after the woman and her husband, but he also realized that this deceitful scheme would impact everyone who would eventually enter the earth through a woman. That would be the entire human race!

All of us entered this world with a sinful nature because of the great fall of the first man and the first woman! One may ask, How is it that I was wrong and in sin before I even arrived on the planet? *The answer is because we all entered the earth with our own self will, compelling us to believe that we must have what we want as God's creation but causing us to rebel against what God wants for our lives as our Creator!* It is not so much that we *did* anything wrong, it was because our *heart* was bent toward our own self-gratification and not bent toward obedience unto God.

However, because God had also created the man with the power of choice, they had the power to choose God and follow His instructions. We can choose to obey God or to disregard Him and lean to our *human reasoning.*

It is within our own power to make the right choice or within our power to choose that which is wrong.

As a woman and a believer, I had to come to terms with a few truths about myself and truths about women in general. What we must realize is that the woman was deceived in the garden, not the man. This is in no way a chauvinistic attack on women at all, for I am one of you—a woman.

Rather it is an enlightenment of who we are. And because of our God-given nature, it is vital that we remain and abide in Christ Jesus and be led by the Holy Spirit so that we are not seduced by the deceiver and tricked. We must realize that Satan's trickery is designed to make us operate on a level less than what God intended.

In addition, we must remember that in Jesus Christ, we are no longer second-class citizens! We are women of equal share, equal authority, equal portion to that which was given to man.

The plot of our enemy, Satan the trickster, is to get us to respond and react on a lower level, a level that is already limited, because it relies totally on our human effort, which ultimately oppresses us. And we never reach our fullest potential that God intended for us as women. Therefore, we, as women, must understand how vital and necessary it is for us to have a daily *working* relationship with Jesus, the Christ! He is the anointed

One, who has given us back our authority, privileges, and our position by His shed blood on the cross!

I am reminded of what Jesus taught in John 15:5: "Yes, I am the vine; you are the branches. Those who remain in me, and I in them, will produce much fruit. For apart from me you can do nothing."

Jesus is the *vine*, and you, meaning all of us, are the *branches*! Without the vine, there are no branches, for the branches are nourished and supplied only by the vine.

When we, as women, the creation of God, operate in any capacity independent from our *Creator*, from our *vine*, it will only be a matter of time before we begin to wither and become unproductive. The scripture assures us, as we continue to read in this chapter, that if we remain in *Him* (Christ Jesus), and His word remains in us, then we are empowered to ask for anything, and it will be granted.

Finally, the authority that was given to us in the garden by our Creator was mismanaged and was given to Satan. *But* in Christ Jesus, we now have it again! He has bought it back! Yes, He has returned it to us! Just as Adam had authority to name every creature in the garden, we now have that same authority, ability, and power, in Jesus's name! In Christ Jesus, we have been reinstated! We have been positioned in our rightful place! We are now eligible to declare God's word over our lives and expect that word to be fruitful and come to pass! We know the truth and will no longer be deceived.

CHAPTER 3

The Woman's Greatest Benefit— Following Instructions

As women of God, we must remind ourselves of how deception was introduced into the earth and how every decision that we are faced with must be in alignment with the Book of Instruction, which is the Word of God. When I consider the fact that God is Creator and that I am one of His created beings, it makes perfect sense that He knows what is best for me. This may seem to be a simple truth, and yet for centuries, man has always tried to function independently of God. Therefore, it is vital for us to *know* the Word of God, which is the *Book of Instruction* and to meditate on His word continually so that we may observe what we need to do.

Study this Book of Instruction continually. Meditate on it day and night so you will be sure to obey everything written in it. Only

then will you prosper and succeed in all you
do. (Josh. 1:8)

We burden ourselves with needless pain and struggles in our lives simply because we refuse to listen to instructions from our Creator. Even in our fallen state, we have come to understand that a malfunctioning vehicle must be returned to the car manufacturer in order to be serviced properly. No one would argue that an ill or sick person usually makes an appointment with their medical doctor for physical checkups in order to feel better. However, we tend to struggle with the fact that as creations of God, we must return to the Creator Himself for all that we need. He is the only one who understands us completely because He created us!

I recall, many years ago, as a very young girl, watching a classic movie *The Wizard of Oz*. I was awestruck as I watched it for the first time around the age of five or six. What I recall and remember more than anything was the prevailing theme of the entire movie, which was, "follow the yellow brick road." That line was repeated often as I sat and stared at the TV screen.

I remember the song that had those words, "follow the yellow brick road." Even at such a young age, I concluded that there would be a happy ending if Dorothy; her little dog, Toto; scarecrow; tin man; and the lion would just do as they had been instructed! I recall that they all arrived in Oz as a result of following the instructions that had been given.

For me, this was the lesson learned from watching that movie so many years ago, and it has always remained with me for all these years.

This movie taught me a valuable life lesson. It taught me that once the goal has been set, it is imperative that I stay focused. If I am pulled away and distracted, my attention is now divided. This is true with all of us. Distractions keep us from functioning at our best, and we are torn. The truth is, whatever holds our attention has mastered us! It can be a person, a place, or a thing.

In the book of Matthew, chapter 6, verse 24, Jesus said, "No man can serve two masters, for either he will hate the one, and love the other; or else he will hold to the one and despise the other." So once again, it comes down to our choice, just as it was in the beginning with the first man, Adam, and the first woman, Eve. We must choose whom we will obey. We must make this decision every day: Whose instructions will I follow? Whose voice will I listen to today? Will I allow the spirit of God to lead me and follow Him, or will I continue to listen to my own carnal and natural instincts?

Let us examine another scripture found in 1 Kings 17:8–12.

> Then the LORD said to Elijah, "Go and
> live in the village of Zarephath, near the city
> of Sidon. I have instructed a widow there to
> feed you." So, he went to Zarephath. As he
> arrived at the gates of the village, he saw a

widow gathering sticks, and he asked her, "Would you please bring me a little water in a cup?" As she was going to get it, he called to her, "Bring me a bite of bread, too."

But she said, "I swear by the LORD your God that I don't have a single piece of bread in the house. And I have only a handful of flour left in the jar and a little cooking oil in the bottom of the jug. I was just gathering a few sticks to cook this last meal, and then my son and I will die."

The prophet Elijah was instructed to travel to a place called Zarephath. He obeyed the instructions, and upon his arrival, he would meet this woman.

This woman had reached the point of poverty, at her very last morsel of food, and had no money. We may view this situation as devastating, but God used it as an opportunity to bless the poor widow woman. Meanwhile, God had already been dealing with her heart and had instructed the woman to sustain him!

Yes, the same woman who was now at the breaking point and one meal away from crossing into poverty, God had selected her to be a blessing to the prophet Elijah.

Take another look here: God selected this woman, someone that is not even mentioned by name. But this is who God selected to change the course of the prophet's life, as well as her own. The scripture shows us that when Elijah obeyed the voice of God and went to the region where he would meet this woman, he requested of her a drink of water. Next, he asked for a cake of bread. The woman knew her situation at home, and she responded to the man of God and informed him that she did not have the resources to prepare a cake of bread, for there was hardly anything for her and her son to eat, But she decided to obey the man of God and prepared what she could with what she had. Not only did she prepare for him, but she also served him first! This woman was an unlikely source for God to use, and yet she received a miracle because she *obeyed the instructions* that the prophet Elijah had given her. She did not allow deception to enter her heart and cause her to miss the blessing of God.

Because this woman obeyed the instructions, she received lasting provision for her household. She *and* her son had more than enough for themselves and to be a blessing to others! This woman had enough faith to follow the instructions that were given to her by the man of God. She didn't dispute his words; she simply obeyed his instruction.

By obeying the prophet of God, she opened the entryway by which God could now use him to bestow blessings upon her life. In doing so, she was positioning herself for God to preserve and to keep her and her household.

Being obedient to the Word of God yields favorable results! When God has designed you to reach your full potential, nothing can stop or detain you if you are obedient to the voice of God and obey His instructions.

When we, as women by God's design, learn to simply trust the Lord with all our heart, we will come to recognize that He is God and that He alone will sustain our lives.

We must realize that every good gift and every perfect gift that we possess has been given to us by God, our Creator. We must always acknowledge the Creator and understand that all of creation is a display of the works of His hands. We must understand that our enemy, Satan, wants to deceive us so that he can derail us. Don't allow this! Follow the instructions, the Word of God.

I have learned that my approach to the Word of God will determine my obedience. What I am saying is this: We must come to a point where the good book or the Holy Bible is not just a decorative item sitting on a nice table, a credenza, or on a desk in our home. It is instead the *book of instruction for my life.* I have come to realize that the volume of that book is filled with instructions. And as I obey them, I prosper. The Word of God is spirit and life. Yes, when you and I approach God's Word with the proper prospective, we will become more receptive and determined to allow those words to change us!

We must remember that God loves us, and His will for us is that we prosper! He desires that we are always above and not beneath. Unfortunately, this was the mistake that Adam and Eve made in the garden. They failed to obey what God had said. They failed to follow the instructions that God had given to them. And upon doing so, they ultimately gave place to the devil.

God wanted them to enjoy the abundant life that He had made available for them. His desire was for them to have fellowship with Him and to give Him worship. His plan for them was to experience the good. He only wanted them to have the best because God's best is His heart for us! God is good, loving, and kind. He desires to give us that which is good.

God wants us to observe, to obey His word, so that we can experience good success! His plan for us is that we love Him, trust Him, and obey His word. As we do so, we make our way successful and prosperous. When we come to the realization that He knows His thoughts and plans for us, we will set our affection on Him. We will seek Him daily for His plans to be revealed unto us. We will desire to stay connected in fellowship with Him so that His plans will unfold in our lives.

I have come to realize too that God's plan unfolds each day. It is not a main event that happens all at once but rather a daily walk, a journey with God. I have come to appreciate the Word of God, and I view it as His instructions to me personally. My perspective about God's instructions has changed. I accept His instructions now as a navigation system or tool for providing guidance. Because when you obey the instructions that have been given by God, you can expect to see the goodness of God manifested in your life, in every area of your life—those areas that are spiritual, as well as those which are natural.

It is vital that we remain obedient to the instructions, the Word of God. They are given to us by God and to keep His Word near to our heart. When we do this, we keep our focus, and our adversary will not be able to deceive us, derail us, nor destroy us.

CHAPTER 4

The Woman's Greatest Influence—the Heart

As I consider many things over the course of my life, I would have to say that as a woman, many of my choices, my desires, my perspectives have many times been motivated by what I could *feel* in my heart. Most women are moved by our feelings, and we carry a lot of emotion from our heart. Many women are usually said to be overly sensitive or emotional. But this is how our Creator designed us, and we are beautifully and wonderfully made!

In fact, I truly believe that God created and designed the woman to be this way for a particular purpose. We are designed to be in touch with another human being more than any other creation. It is a woman after all, who are the incubators of human life! I don't consider this as a curse but instead a blessing. I believe that a woman by God's design is the woman who is capable of feeling tenderness and warmth. She is also discerning and compassionate. This woman shows concern and empathy for others and very capable of demonstrating the love of God. It is that deep caring and nurturing component of every woman's being that makes us who we are as women. We are sentimental, and there is no shame in that. We care because God designed us this way. We are most vulnerable because we easily allow ourselves to be moved with feelings of tenderness and affection, which causes us to love like our Heavenly Father because He loves us greatly and tenderly.

A heart that is turned toward God is a powerful heart! This is a heart that will be pliable, touchable, and ready for use by our Heavenly Father.

This is the heart that God can and will connect with because this heart, the heart of the woman, is open and receptive. It is important to mention also that as women, we must make certain that our hearts trust in the Lord. It is He who will help us to guard and keep our heart when we trust Him. We must allow Him to teach us how to keep our heart with all diligence, for out of it springs the issues of life. The scripture in Proverbs 21:2 says, "Every way of a man is right in his own eyes, but the Lord examines the heart." Our hearts are as fragile as glass and yet as strong as iron. Our heart knows the answers many times long before the mind comprehends, and yet that same heart can be broken into many pieces. Our heart holds our dreams of the future, as well as our memories of the past. It stores up both our joy, as well as our pain. The heart of a woman can be easily touched, as well as tormented. God has promised that when we acknowledge Him with all our heart, He will direct our path. He has also promised that when we delight in Him, He will give us the desires of our heart.

Let us be reminded that at the initial acceptance of Jesus, our Savior and Lord, our heart was involved. In Romans 10:9–10, the scripture states "that if we would confess with our mouth the Lord Jesus *and* believe in our *heart* that God raised Him from the dead, we would be saved!" The heart had to believe what the mouth confessed for us to be born again into the family of God. We have been designed in such a way that what we speak from our mouth reveals what we hold in our heart. When the heart holds good treasure, it will speak that which is good.

Also, in the book of First Samuel, chapter 16, verses 6–7, it states, "When they arrived, Samuel took one look at Eliab and thought, 'Surely this is the LORD's anointed!' But the LORD said to Samuel, 'Don't judge by his appearance or height, for I have rejected him. The LORD doesn't see things the way you see them. People judge by outward appearance, but the LORD looks at the heart.'"

I wanted us to see this scripture because we see how God sees. As the Lord God spoke to the prophet Samuel in search of the next king of Israel, God instructed him not to focus on the height and physical stature of a potential candidate. But instead, God wanted Samuel to pay attention to the *heart* of the potential candidate because this is what the Lord sees. God sees our heart. A heart that is filled with the love of God, the mercy of God, and the compassion of God is a heart after God's own heart!

When we, as women, allow the Holy Spirit to encompass our very being and remain steadfast in the teachings of Scripture, our hearts will be changed, and our minds will be renewed. This is the woman that God is searching for in the earth. He desires the woman to feel what He feels and to love as He loves!

That is the beauty that lies within every woman—a woman by God's design. This woman realizes that her beauty is not limited to the physical structure of her body. She understands that the body is temporal and constantly changing day by day.

Although she is aware of her physical body, she also understands, I am not my body, and my body is not me. I am a spirit, I possess a soul, and I live in a body. I reflect God's love and am influenced by His spirit within me.

The book of Proverbs, chapter 31, verses 10–12 states, "Who can find a virtuous and capable woman? She is more precious than rubies. Her husband can trust her, and she will greatly enrich his life. She brings him good, not harm, all the days of her life."

These verses begin with a question, asking, Who can find this woman? This woman is a priceless jewel! She is one that is rare, which makes her very precious. We see that this woman is like no other. As you continue to read this chapter from verses 13–31, you will read that her husband's heart trusts in her because he knows that she has his best interest at heart, her heart! He recognizes that she is trustworthy.

This woman by God's design is not a woman that can be found everywhere because she is a rare and precious treasure. This virtuous woman, who is designed by God, although she is rare, she will stand out in a crowd. She is not seen as obnoxious because she stands out, but rather her quiet inner beauty speaks well on her behalf. She takes pride in her outward appearance, but it is her gentleness and comforting nature that is captivating to others. The glory of God that she is surrounded in totally embraces her. When she opens her mouth, her words are wise, strong, and yet very gentle. She indeed is a woman by God's design, who has a heart for God.

She is a smart woman who concerns herself with her husband, her family, and the good of others. She seeks out the raw materials, which is the very best needed in order to construct garments for her household. She doesn't think or believe that she is more than who she is, but at the same time, she demonstrates great pride in what she brings to her family. She serves them with gladness, and everything that she does is done from a heart of pure and genuine concern and love for them.

Yes, she is a woman by God's design, a woman who knows her worth and yet does not flaunt it in any way. She demonstrates her worth by making certain that those that she loves feel worthy themselves. She is encouraging and supportive to those in her family.

This woman is also an astute businesswoman. She understands how to negotiate and is resourceful. She takes time to make decisions and doesn't allow herself to do so on an impulse!

This demonstrates her ability to sit down and count the cost before jumping headlong into a business deal. She takes time to make decisions. She gives thought to her steps as she strives to do all things in the spirit of excellence.

She is a woman who knows how to plan, organize, and execute those plans well. She is a strategic planner, and everything that she does is purposeful. We see this virtuous woman as one who considers a field and buys it. Yes, this woman is intelligent and aware of a profitable business deal when she sees it.

She also understands the importance of having a rhythm to her life. She is one who awakes early in the morning to begin her daily tasks. She is a smart woman. She understands sowing and reaping; therefore, she plants a vineyard and expects to see a harvest come forth.

A woman by God's design is a woman that realizes, her wealth and gains are the result of her laboring, planting, and sowing seed. She does not wait for others to bring to her and to serve her, although she herself has maidens.

No! She realizes that she is responsible for her own well-being, and she knows how to care for herself and for everyone around her.

Verse 17 says that this woman equips herself with strength. How? You may ask.

She relies on the Lord God to be her strength, her fortress, her strong tower. She does not depend upon others to bring to her what she needs. She can move out in the strength of God and equips herself spiritually, mentally, physically, and emotionally. A woman by God's design is confident in her decisions because she seeks the Lord and His wisdom. And because she does so, she feels assured whenever she must decide about anything in her life.

This woman is a soldier. She is strong, competent, and loyal to her family. A woman by God's design can be strict when necessary, unbreakable when tested, and very hardworking for the sake of her family. Yet at the same time, she is graceful and more beautiful than a pearl!

She manages and is involved with every aspect of her life and does not totally depend upon others to give her happiness. She instead allows herself to be used as a willing vessel to bring others happiness in their lives. As a result of her heart motives, she herself is blessed with all good things. A woman by God's design wears strength, dignity, and honor, and even her husband praises her. Her children also see her as blessed of the Lord.

When a woman by God's design allows her heart to be pliable and conformable unto the hand of God, she becomes invincible.

She will not be defeated or overcome by anything, for she understands that in God, she moves, lives, and has her being! She moves in alignment with His spirit and brings refreshment to everyone and everything in her life path.

She is a woman by God's design, and her presence is felt and known by all. This cwoman is a strong being because her heart doth trust in the Lord, her God.

CHAPTER 5

The Woman's Greatest Memories—Childhood

Many of our decisions and viewpoints are often established in our childhood. It is during this time in our lives that we are most impressionable. We begin to learn so many emotions from a very young age. Research has shown that a young girl that is attended to well usually feels more secure as a young adult. By the same token, a baby girl who cried for some attention to be given but was often neglected learns to self-soothe. That child becomes very familiar with emotions, such as rejection and abandonment at a very young age. This child will probably experience bouts of shyness and fear because it needs validation in order to feel confident about itself.

Too often, children don't receive the care and nurturing that they deserve and are left to protect and care for themselves. All of this will negatively affect their lives, not only as young children but in their adulthood as well.

Many women spend a lifetime emotionally and spiritually asleep and not enthused because they don't understand their purpose.

It is like sleepwalking through your entire life! You spend endless days and nights trying to decide what your life is all about. It is not until we return to our Creator that we understand who we are as His creation. It is then, and only then, that we discover what He already knows about us. We were preordained and equipped with gifts, talents, and abilities.

It has always been intriguing to me when I read the scripture from the book of Isaiah 46:10.

> Only I can tell you the future before it
> even happens.
> Everything I plan will come to pass for I
> do whatever I wish.

It is God alone who can reveal our life paths unto us. God has already preordained the path that we would walk in. I find this so captivating. It is important that we realize and understand that God is a purposeful being. God planned you, and nobody else can be like you. God is not a duplicator; He is a Creator. Each of us must embrace this truth about ourselves.

This is true of every living human being on this planet. God designed each of us cynd equipped us with His purpose and His plan for our journey on this earth. To know this excites me that I am a woman by God's design!

I can now see the hand of God as I look back over my life. Even before I understood my existence, God already knew me. I understand more clearly the sovereignty of God.

It was God in His infinite wisdom who planned the genetic makeup of my very being and purposed that the egg of my mother and the sperm of my father would conceive a female child. It was He who sealed that conception in place, and my life cycle began. It was God who also decided exactly when that process would end nine months later, giving me a birth date of October 19. How? Because just like He knew the prophets of old, He knew me before I was conceived in my mother's womb!

As I reflect on my childhood years, I must acknowledge that I grew up in a loving home with two nurturing parents. I was their only child and their pride and joy. Most of my memories of my childhood were pleasant ones that I have always cherished. I recall my parents always wanting to do things as a family, so I never felt left out. They were hardworking people who took pride in their work and managed to build a good home for me. I have many fond memories of being a young girl, and I loved to hang out with my daddy! He was a truck driver during the time and would make trips delivering concrete products to new construction sites. We would rise early in the morning and get the day started. Seat belts were not enforced back then, so I loved climbing up into this eighteen-wheeler tractor trailer and sit next to my daddy on my special seat. Daddy had constructed it so that I could sit tall and see over the dashboard. We made many trips together in the mountains of the Carolinas, Virginia, and a few times to Tennessee. I am sure, those times spent with Daddy were special to him as well. I always loved taking those trips with him! When I was old enough to attend kindergarten, the trips with Daddy slowed down. I truly missed going with him, for I loved to ride along! There were a few times he would have to make a trip on weekends, but it was very rare. The times that he did travel on weekends, I would go along. By the time I reached first grade, I was unable to ride along with him anymore. I enjoyed my elementary school years, participating in the school play when I was in third grade, being the captain of our school safety patrol, and playing the flutophone in the fourth and fifth grade. Oh, how I loved that! I recall being a part of the North Carolina Symphony because our school would go to the NCCU college campus each year and be a part of an entire group of fourth and fifth graders across the state coming together to play our flutophones. That was the most fun field trip for me as a young girl! Outside of the school fun, there was family fun trips as well. Each year we would travel to our family reunion, and there I would unite with all my relatives on my father's side of the family. All of us kids would have such a great time playing games, eating good food, and drinking all the lemonade and soda pops we could hold! My parents had this date on their calendar year after year. When it was over, we all would hug one another and look forward to the next year to do it all over again! I always enjoyed being around family.

My childhood home was a place filled with Southern hospitality. My mother was an excellent cook, and she always had homemade cake and sweet tea to offer anyone who would stop by for a visit. Those two items were a staple in our home. If you were invited for Sunday dinner, you were in for a delicious meal! My mother would cook so much food. She always wanted each guest to have food options, so she prepared more than enough to ensure that they would. She would prepare everything from the main course to the desserts. The table would be filled with guests and plenty of delicious food! It was just a part of who she was as she loved to show hospitality and loved feeding people. There would be plenty of conversation, laughter, and a well-spent Sunday afternoon. It wasn't a strange thing to see a few folk nodding and napping on couches and chairs after enjoying such a hearty meal!

I would say that my fondest childhood memory of all was going to the NC State Fair. Each year the event would take place in the fall.

The window of time would be for ten days, and one of those days would include my birthday. As a special treat, my father would take me and several neighborhood children to the state fair. There would be at least eight kids in the car, me included. It was like having a road trip birthday party all in one! When we would arrive at the fair, my father would pair us up in twos and tell us to stay together. He then would find a bench and sit and wait several hours until we all had exhausted ourselves on the rides and filled up with all the hotdogs and cotton candy that we could eat! It became a birthday tradition, and I always looked forward to going. My childhood memories are happy ones that I will always cherish.

Around the time I was ten years old, I remember one hot summer day, after playing outside, I decided to go inside to rest. My mother was in the kitchen. And as I was making myself a glass of cold water, I commented to her that while being outside, there had been a boy whom I had seen in our neighborhood from time to time standing across the street from our house. While I was outside, He had waved at me quite eagerly, and I waved back reluctantly. I mentioned this to my mother, and she asked if I knew his name. I responded, "Yes, his name is Harold." I had not had any conversations with him, but I would hear other people calling him by that name. I continued to tell her that "sometimes, when I am walking home from the bus stop or at the corner store, he would always say hello or wave to me."

I knew that he was older than I was and wasn't sure why he seemed to make a point of getting my attention.

My mother turned and looked at me with a smile. She then said, "Let's sit at the table for a little," so we did. I sat down and begin to drink the cold water that I had poured for myself. She began to explain the reason she believed that Harold was probably giving me attention. She went on to say that "Harold is your brother."

At that moment, I had just taken a sip of water, which was in my mouth. But upon hearing those words, I remember opening my mouth, and all the water gushed out! I sat very still for several minutes, trying to process what she had just said. She asked, "Are you okay? Did you hear what I said?" And then I responded, "My brother?" She said, "Yes, he is your brother." Then I asked, "Why doesn't he live with us if he is my brother?" And then the next three words that she said to me, I will never forget, for they were as astonishing as what she had said before. She said, "You were adopted. I did not birth you, but I love you just as my very own child."

At that moment, as a ten-year-old, I wasn't sure what to feel, what to say, or even what to think! I stayed seated at the table and was quiet for several minutes. I don't know how long I sat there, but it felt like a long time. In my young mind, I was trying to interpret exactly what she meant, and nothing made sense. My mother then said, "I have been waiting for the right time to explain everything to you, and now is that time." She then asked me a question. "Do you remember those times I took you to visit Miss Annis?" I thought for a minute and responded, "Yes." She then said, "She is your mother. "She is the woman that birthed you."

After hearing this, I was very baffled and confused. I was speechless. It felt as though my entire body had just gone limp. In the next few moments, I seemed to have gone into a zone and wasn't really paying much attention to anything else that was said. She placed her hand on my hand and squeezed it gently, and she began to recall the day that I came into her life.

She relived the story as she was telling it to me. She started by saying that at the time, she and my daddy lived in a duplex apartment further down the street. She remembered being out in her backyard on this spring day because she was doing the laundry and was hanging clothes on the line to dry. As she was doing so, her next-door neighbor stuck her head from her back door to let mother know that someone had just gone inside of her house.

At this point, as she hurriedly climbed the back porch steps and opened the screen door, she could see something on the bed but wasn't able to determine what it was. She continued walking toward the bedroom. And as she approached the bed, she realized that whatever was on the bed was moving slightly! The closer she got to her bed; she realized it was a baby!—yes, a baby, a little girl wrapped in a light blanket and wearing a mildly wet diaper with a half-filled bottle of milk. That little baby girl was me! She said she had guessed me to be around seven months old at the time.

She mentioned also that next to me was a couple of faded t-shirts and another bottle filled with water, and all these items had been placed inside of a brown paper bag.

She was shocked to see me and had no idea who I was or where I had come from. She ran to the front door to see if there was anyone walking or driving away outside that could help her to understand what had just happened. She recalled that day, the street was totally clear. There were no vehicles passing, neither was there anyone cwalking on the sidewalk. In fact, she recalled it was peacefully still at the time.

She came back in, rushed into the bedroom, picked me up, and stood there in total shock, holding me in her arms, trying to figure out who I was, where the mother was, and how she ended up with me. Her head was totally spinning with so many thoughts. She had so many questions and yet no answers. She described that moment as being totally dumbfounded and feeling helpless!

She immediately called her husband's job and left a message for him to return the call as soon as possible. During this time, because he was a truck driver, he was usually out on the road most of the day, so she didn't expect him to call very soon. She completely stopped doing her chores and decided to finish the laundry and tidy up the house later. She decided to run quickly to the next-door neighbor's apartment and was knocking frantically on the door.

When the neighbor finally came to the door, she began to tell her what had happened. The neighbor and my mother returned to her apartment, and the neighbor picked me up. At that point, they both thought it would be a good idea to walk around the neighborhood to see if anyone recognized my face, and hopefully, that would begin to answer some of the questions in her head.

As they started walking down the sidewalk, they saw another neighbor outside, working in her yard. She stated that she did remember seeing me with a woman several days before and thought that probably was my mother. Neither of these two neighbors really knew my birth mother and wasn't sure where she lived.

From that point, both women continued to walk along with my mother, trying to locate my birth mother, which was no easy task.

After walking, searching, and knocking on doors about two hours or more and asking several people about her whereabouts, they finally learned that the birth mother had most likely left the neighborhood.

They also learned that the birth mother sometimes visited the neighborhood because she was a friend to a couple that lived nearby. She then learned that this couple were both working folk, but usually returned home around 6:00 p.m. My mother decided to wait around a little longer, but she knew she would need to leave and possibly return the next day to speak with the couple.

She and the two other neighbors made their way back to their homes as the evening was approaching.

She did not receive a call back from her husband, but he did get back home at the usual time that evening, around 5:30 p.m. When he arrived, she was sitting in a chair, holding me, and he walked in, looked at her in total astonishment, and then asked, "What is that?" She looks up at her husband and responded, "A little baby girl." She instructed him to sit at the dining table while she prepared his plate, and then they would talk. During the conversation that evening, she recalled that her husband had made it emphatically clear that he did not want to keep this baby! He insisted that they take me to some agency downtown, like the police or fire department, and be rid of me, but the woman who would become my mother just couldn't seem to part ways with me. Over several days, she said she prayed for guidance, and she and her husband continued to discuss everything in detail.

The days and nights would come and go. Still no one had seen or heard from the birth mother. And by this time, one week had gone by. She had thought, by this time, the birth mother would have returned to pick me up or perhaps tried to contact her, but it never happened. By now, she said she and her husband had decided to do some shopping for items that I would need.

The following Saturday morning, they went to Sears and shopped for a baby crib, clothes, shoes, and all the supplies that babies need. Of course, as the days continued to pass, her husband was becoming more attached to me himself and loved me as his own. However, he still had some reluctance because of the concern that the birth mother could return at any time and take me away, and he was concerned that something like that would be devastating to his wife! But this lady, the woman who was to be my mother, was not hearing any of it!

She stated that she had been pregnant about five months before all of this occurred, and she was devastated after experiencing a miscarriage. So having me in her life, even if only for a brief period, was very meaningful to her. She then recalled that she had finally been able to connect with the neighbor who knew my birth mother. After speaking with that neighbor, she now understood how my birth mother had learned about her. That neighbor had told my birth mother that she knew of a couple who would love to have a child, and that they had recently miscarried. With that information, my birth mother had made the decision to leave me as she had done.

She continued with the story and told me that on Sunday, after we all woke up and had breakfast, she and my father began to prepare to attend Sunday morning worship. Attending church was a custom in their household and remained that way all through my childhood years. She began to laugh when she shared this part of the story as she recalled pleasant memories. She said that as she was trying to get me dressed, I was busy undressing myself! She would put on a sock, and I would take it off. She would put on a shoe, and I would pull that off! She said that she placed a pretty silk ribbon on my hair, and I would reach up and snatch it right off. Whatever she would put on, I would immediately pull off!

She chuckled out loud while recollecting that part of the story. She said that it took both her and my father to dress me for church that Sunday and many Sundays thereafter! He would have to hold my hands while she put my clothes on.

Finally, we were all dressed and ready to go by 10:45, and off to church we would go! After church services, the pastor and his wife visited for the afternoon. It was then that she mentioned how I watched her every move while she was preparing the meal. She said the pastor's wife told her that "this baby is watching you because she knows you will be her mother." After finishing the cooking and cleaning of dinner plates, the pastor's wife told her that she should keep me because I needed a good home. She mentioned how well I had eaten that day and how she discovered I loved potatoes! The pastor's wife had mashed a few in a saucer and fed me, and I ate every morsel she recalled.

She continued with her story and told me that she remembered, I never cried. I had not cried at all. She had a smile on her face when she recalled that each morning, I would wake up and lie in my crib very quietly and play with my feet. She said I was always very peaceful and content. When she shared that with me, it was then that I cried! We both shed tears at that moment.

After wiping away tears, I began to feel a lot of emotions.

I could not identify exactly what I felt, but I knew I felt something. Perhaps it was a myriad of emotions, ranging from being surprised to feeling detached.

I had now learned of my beginnings, as well as learning about a brother, whose name was Harold, all in one day! That was quite a big deal for a ten-year-old who only went into the house for a glass of cold water!

A few weeks later, my adoptive mother and I went to visit Miss Annis as we would do from time to time. Miss Annis came to the door and welcomed us into her home. She spoke to me in her same usual way and invited me and my mother in. After they greeted each other, Miss Annis commented that I looked so pretty and that she liked my dress.

I don't recall what my response was because I was still processing all this information. I do remember looking at her face a little longer this time and listening to her voice a little more carefully this time. *So this is my birth mother*, I thought to myself.

It all was so overwhelming. Miss Annis told me that the children were all outside playing, and I could go out and join them if I wanted to. Usually, when we would go there, the children would be outside, so that was nothing new. Only this time, these weren't just "the children." I was processing all this new information, and it became clear to me that if these children were her children, that made them my siblings! These children were my brothers and sisters! Suddenly, I didn't really want to play with anyone or go outside! I just wanted to be quiet and be still. After sitting still for a few minutes, my mom asked if I was feeling okay, and I said I was not and asked if we were going home soon. She said, "Okay, we will leave in a few minutes."

On the way home, she asked me again if I was feeling okay, and I said, "Yes," but inside I wasn't sure what to say or how to even feel anymore. I recalled being very quiet, and my mother knew that I was not exactly myself. When we returned home, I went to my room and tried to gather myself. She came into my room, pulled up a chair, and asked, "What is wrong with you?" I couldn't respond; I just remember starting to cry. As I reflect on it, it was like sobbing. I had so much pinned-up emotion inside! She pulled me close and held me in her arms and said, "Stop crying. There is no reason to cry, and everything will be all right."

I felt so much better after she spoke those words to me. I was too young to understand my feelings back at the time, but her words reassured me that everything was okay. As time passed and I matured, I thanked God that my adoptive mother had given me the truth about my life.

She had wanted me to know my beginnings and wanted me to "know my people." I realized, it took a lot of courage for my mother to tell me my history. It was a totally unselfish act on her part. Often, adopted children are never told the truth about their origin, and yet it is a part of who we are. It is our history. All of us have history, and none of us had anything to do with it.

It is our story, but it is not one that we wrote. None of us have anything to do with where we came from, but all of us have a voice in where we're going.

I came to realize that she and her husband, the man who eventually became my adoptive father, had a choice. They could have easily taken me to a police or fire station and left me there. As I continued to reflect over this part of my life, I could see the hand of God involved in every step and every decision! Yes, God had ordered my footsteps. God was paving the way for me—yes, me. It was God's design that I would become a part of their family and be raised by them. It took several years before my adoption was legal due to having to change attorneys a few times and broken communication issues between my parents and social workers. But my adoptive mother was a fighter, and she would not surrender until this battle was over! Today, I have all those documents in my possession, and I appreciate the very paper that they were typed on because of what it stands for! It is a part of my story, my life, my history.

Looking back, I know that God had His hand upon my life, even as an infant! What was awesome to me was that even when I did not know Him, He knew me. Even when I was unable to speak a word to Him, He spoke on my behalf to Mr. and Mrs. McKoy! He touched their hearts and gave them a desire to want to love me as their very own child.

Although my beginnings were a little unsettled, God had been involved in my life all my life! I was fortunate enough to have spent my childhood with parents that truly loved, nurtured, and provided for me. The faithfulness of God was clearly seen in that He intended for me to be placed in a home so that I would be provided for in the best possible way. God, in His infinite wisdom, already knew who I would become.

> He knows the thoughts that he thinks
> towards us and plans that He has for each of
> us, thoughts of peace, *not* of evil, to give us an
> expected end. (Jer. 29:11)

I am reminded of the scripture in Ephesians 1:4–6.

> According as he hath chosen us in him
> before the foundation of the world, that we
> should be holy and without blame before

him in love: Having predestinated us unto the adoption of children by Jesus Christ to himself, according to the good pleasure of his will, To the praise of the glory of his grace, wherein he hath made us accepted in the beloved.

These scriptures speak to me in a deeper way now because of my beginnings in this life. They clearly reveal to me that God has given each of us the option to be a part of His family through Jesus! Because of Him, we no longer need to remain in a fallen state because of sin, because God has already predestined and *adopted* us and made provision for us to be received into His family and to be accepted by Him!

The remaining part of my history that I learned later was that my brother Harold had also been adopted by another couple that lived in the same neighborhood. After learning that he was my brother, I would be happy when I would see him around, and we would chat briefly on occasion. Unfortunately, after some time had passed, Harold was drafted into the US Army and killed in the Vietnam War.

I am grateful today that God also allowed me to meet and spend time with many of my older siblings that I had not known about while growing up.

We have lost a few in death over the years, but those of us that remain are still in contact with one another to this day.

Today, I can look back and thank God as a woman, mother, and grandmother, for all that *He* has done. I pay tribute to both my mothers who were placed into my life, my birth mother, who loved me enough to give me away, and my adoptive mother, who loved me enough to keep me!

CHAPTER 6

The Woman's Greatest Motivation— to Encourage Others

I believe that each woman carries within herself beauty; however, many times, we are not aware of that. We all contain and hold precious spiritual treasure within us that oftentimes is buried deep down within, under the pain and the hurt, the rejection, and the abandonment to the point we feel that we have nothing and lose our sense of value, until God connects us to another person, that special connection that brings out the very best of who we are.

One of the greatest joys that any woman can experience is to have a close *earthly* friend!—a sister. She may be one that is *related* by blood because she shares the same parents as you do, or she could be one who is *relatable* because she shares your views and is considered a friend. In both cases, a relationship like this is very special indeed because you have that support and comradery that bonds you to one another!

You grow to appreciate each other, respect each other, and trust each other. You know that this sister will support you, stand by you, and more importantly, she will tell you the truth. She will be the keeper of all your secrets, as well as your concerns. She will remain calm when you are upset. She will rejoice when you rejoice and even weep when you weep.

Mary, the mother of Jesus, had this connection with her relative, Elizabeth. The two women shared a bond between them that was supernatural. As I meditated on their connection, I could see how God strategically aligned their lives together at the perfect time for *His* purpose.

Elizabeth and her husband had lived a righteous life in the sight of God. However, the one thing that they desired was to have a child.

Elizabeth was barren and had not been able to conceive. She and her husband had gotten very old.

> And they had no child, because that
> Elisabeth was barren, and they both were
> now well stricken in years. (Luke 1:7)

In Luke 1:5–6, we begin to read the story of Elizabeth, who was the wife of Zachariah, a priest.

> There was in the days of Herod, the king
> of Judaea, a certain priest named Zacharias,
> of the course of Abia: and his wife was of

the daughters of Aaron, and her name was
Elisabeth. And they were both righteous
before God, walking in all the command-
ments and ordinances of the Lord blameless

One day, while Zachariah was performing his usual duties
in the temple, he was visited by an angel of the Lord, who
announced to him that he and his wife would have a son! Of
course he was overwhelmed by this announcement. But by
God's power, Elizabeth did conceive a child in her golden years!
During this same time, Mary had been visited by an angel of
the Lord. The angel had spoken to her and delivered unto her
the message of God, stating that she had found favor in God's
sight and had been chosen to carry the Savior, our Lord Jesus!
Upon hearing all this, Mary gave her consent in Luke 1:38.

And Mary said, Behold the handmaid
of the Lord; be it unto me according to thy
word. And the angel departed from her.

Mary then traveled to the home of Elizabeth and, unbe-
knownst to her, Elizabeth was also with child. When Mary
arrived at her home, she greeted her, and at the very sound of
Mary's voice, Elizabeth's child leaped within her womb! At that
very moment, Elizabeth began to give God praise because she
then knew that Mary was also pregnant.

She entered the house and greeted Elizabeth.

At the sound of Mary's greeting, Elizabeth's child leaped within her, and Elizabeth was filled with the Holy Spirit. (Luke 1:40–41)

It is important to understand here that everything is made beautiful in its own time. God knows when that time is, for He is our Creator. One may ask, why did Elizabeth have to wait so long before she conceived a child? And yet on the other hand, Mary was quite young when she was appointed to conceive Jesus. The response to both is God's timing! We must understand that God operates in the realm of eternity, and we operate in the realm of time. He is God, and He alone knows the perfect time for everything that concerns us! God, in His infinite wisdom, has strategically placed every part of our lives into His timing! The beauty of this story of these two women is that when Elizabeth heard the voice of Mary, the child within her responded with a leap!

We can see that the beauty of sisterhood is that when a woman who is in fellowship with God, and His spirit connects with another woman who is also in fellowship with God and His spirit, something supernatural occurs.

Something comes alive in each of us! The spiritual womb of every born-again woman is full of life, full of hidden treasure that are waiting to be manifested! It was Elizabeth who was overcome by the Holy Spirit, and she began to speak over the life of Mary. It gave Elizabeth much joy to be used of God to encourage and bless her friend Mary.

She was honored that Mary, who had been chosen to be the mother of Jesus, had come to visit her!

> Elizabeth gave a glad cry and exclaimed to Mary, "God has blessed you above all women, and your child is blessed. I am so honored, that the mother of my Lord should visit me. When I heard your greeting, the baby in my womb jumped for joy. You are blessed because you believed that the Lord would do what he said." (Luke 1:42–45)

She was rejoicing with Mary! She was excited for Mary. This is what sisters do. There are times when we, as women, can become oppressed, and we may feel isolated and unsure of many things. But when we get in fellowship with our sisters and experience that love and support, everything changes. Perhaps Elizabeth may have felt this at one point before she had conceived John. She was a much older woman than her cousin Mary, but God saw fit to use both the older, more seasoned, mature woman, as well as the younger, youthful and vibrant, and willing woman. God made the decision to use both women because *He* is God, and He knows the end from the beginning.

He alone knows what His will is to be for our lives, and therefore, we must trust God's timing and God's purpose.

> To everything there is a season, and a
> time to every purpose under the heaven.
> (Eccles. 3:1)

I know that when women make this connection with one another, it empowers us! It makes us greater and stronger. We understand one another in a more intimate way. We begin to see that our shared experiences make us relatable as sisters!

Women have been given these special qualities to nurture one another and to really feel heartfelt concern for one another. We then understand how to be a source of encouragement and strength to each other.

All of this is supernatural and has been given to us by God.

Our souls become intertwined, and we begin to speak the same thing, hope for the same thing, and we are perfectly joined together in the same mind.

First Corinthians 1:10 says, "Now I beseech you, brethren, by the name of our Lord Jesus Christ, that ye all speak the same thing, and that there be no divisions among you; but that ye be perfectly joined together in the same mind and in the same judgment."

There is a very powerful force at work when women become one in the spirit. We are immovable, unshakable, and fearful of nothing. Every born-again woman of God has been given a purpose that lies deep within.

She is incubating and carrying something good inside! When we can provide support and encouragement to one another, we are being productive. We come together as one body, life-giving to life-giving, and what a supernatural power that is! We can give birth to all those things that God has blessed us with and be a blessing to others! When we can stand together and lift each other in prayer, we are giving life! When we can listen and understand each other, we are nurturing! The woman by God's design comes to realize that she is a fruit bearer.

She understands that God designed her to encourage, support, bring life, nurture, and strengthen another woman.

We are stronger when we do this because that is how God designed us. We should not be concerned that we will run out of supply, for God will always supply and give us the resources that we may need to do His will. I also need to bring to your attention how important it is to see the timing of God. Elizabeth, the older woman, had waited for many years to conceive and to give birth. She probably had given up on the idea. But God, who is perfect in all His ways, had a plan. During the time that she was waiting, Mary, who was a young child, was growing up somewhere in Nazareth, had also been appointed by God to be the mother of Jesus. However, Mary had to grow up and mature as a young woman in order to bring the manifestation of God's plan to maturity.

In other words, Elizabeth was patiently waiting to conceive, while Mary was actively growing and maturing into a young woman.

In the plan of God, He had already predesignated and knew that Elizabeth would bear a son, and that son would become John the Baptist. God also knew that John would be the forerunner for our Lord and Savior, Jesus.

Likewise, God also knew that Mary would bear a son, and He would be the Messiah! His name would be Jesus, the Savior of the world, born of a virgin.

It would be John the Baptist who would be the forerunner of Jesus and would prepare the way of the Lord.

> And you, my little son, will be called the prophet of the Highest, because you will prepare the way for the Lord. You will tell his people how to find salvation through forgiveness of their sins. Because of God's tender mercy, the morning light from heaven is about to break upon us, to give light to those who sit in darkness and in the shadow of death, and to guide us to the path of peace."
> (Luke 1:76–79)

God already had preordained and foreplaned the perfect time in history when the two of these sons would be conceived and be born into the earth. To everything there is a season and a time for every purpose under the heaven. It is not by chance or by might or by coincidence that people meet when they meet. It is by the will of God that he has ordered our footsteps, and our lives connect in God's timing. Sometimes we may not fully understand what God is doing at the time He is moving. We may even be overtaken with the spirit of fear and become apprehensive, but that is when we must trust our God. We must come to that place of understanding that God leads us in small steps, little by little. As sisters and women by God's design, we can encourage one another with this truth and support one another. We are not placed on this earth for everyone, but we are placed here for someone. I believe that God has qualified each of us to be a perfect solution to someone. As a woman by God's design, we should look for opportunities to heal, strengthen, and bless others when it is within our power to do so! When we understand and know that everything works together to our advantage when we trust God, we will be able to encourage one another with those words! We must be assured that our footsteps have been ordered by the Lord. He knows the path that we should take, and He leads us into those paths as it pleases Him. He does not unfold our entire life before our eyes, but He does gently lead us as little children. God knows how to orchestrate every detail of our lives and to bring His perfect will into manifestation in His own time. So we say, as Mary, the mother of Jesus, readily received the message of the angel and said, "Behold the handmaid of the Lord; be it unto me according to thy word" (Luke 1:38).

CHAPTER 7

The Woman's Greatest Fear—Change

Each one of us has a certain amount of hesitation when it comes to change, and yet change is inevitable. It is constant and can't be avoided because the very nature of change demonstrates to us that it is transitional! Though we pride ourselves to think that we enjoy and accept change in our lives, most people do not welcome it.

Change is different, change is uncomfortable, and change is also unknown. As human beings, we tend to resist those elements in our lives: different, uncomfortable, and unknown. In fact, these are the same elements that often prevent us from reaching out to others. We find that we hesitate to approach others because they are different. We allow those differences to cause us to feel uncomfortable. Afterward, we realize that we have ventured into an unknown territory.

God's desire is that, in those times, we use the measure of faith that He has given each of us to open our hearts and allow ourselves to experience new adventures with Him. We serve a big God, who is the Creator of heaven and earth. The earth is the Lord's *and* the fullness thereof the world and they that dwell therein. When we understand this truth, it will motivate us to go wherever the spirit of God should lead us without fear and without hesitation. I am reminded of the prophet Elijah, a man of God, who had the privilege to see the hand of God in his life on many occasions.

In 1 Kings 17, beginning at verse 2, God instructed the prophet Elijah to leave where he was and to go to another location. Change!

> Then the LORD said to Elijah, "Go to the east and hide by Cherith Brook, near where it enters the Jordan River. Drink from the brook and eat what the ravens bring you, for I have commanded them to bring you food."

We must point out here that God was specific in His instructions and directed the man of God to a certain location *by the brook Cherith.* He also told Elijah in verse 4 that He had commanded the ravens to sustain him in that place! Look at the hand of God! He is the Creator of the universe and has control over His creation! God uses whom and what He wills to be a resource to us as necessary! A raven is an unlikely source, and yet God, in His infinite power, caused this creature to be a blessing to the prophet.

The prophet obeyed the instructions and went to the *exact* location that God had instructed. After a season of time had passed, the Word of the Lord came to Elijah again. In verse 8, he was instructed to change! The Lord commanded him to go to another location, Zarephath, and again God had already prepared for his provision in that place also. The scripture says that God had commanded a widow woman to sustain and provide for Elijah.

> Then the LORD said to Elijah, "Go and live in the village of Zarephath, near the city of Sidon. I have instructed a widow there to feed you." So, he went to Zarephath. (1 Kings 17:8–10)

Again, the man of God obeyed the instructions that he had received.

Each time, the prophet Elijah was instructed to go to a specific location and be provided for by a specific source. As a woman by God's design, this is a very important wisdom key. It is important to understand that wherever God leads us, He will provide and take care of us in that place. As a woman by God's design, we must seek Him for His guidance in our lives so that we are always in the exact place where we should be and not where we *think* we should be. We must realize that we were created for a specific place, as well as a specific purpose. We must accept the fact that we are not created for everyone, but we are created for someone. Just as Eve was created for Adam, you and I are someone's reward. Each of us are a reward to a specific person. Our provision will not be identical to another sister's provision, but it will be provision just the same. I am reminded of the scripture in Matthew 7:7–10, where we are instructed to ask, seek, and knock.

> Keep on asking, and you will receive what you ask for. Keep on seeking, and you will find. Keep on knocking, and the door will be opened to you. For everyone who asks, receives. Everyone who seeks, finds. And to everyone who knocks, the door will be opened. "You parents—if your children ask for a loaf of bread, do you give them a stone instead? Or if they ask for a fish, do you give them a snake? Of course not!

These scriptures assure that when we ask, we will receive. When we seek, we will find, and when we knock the door will be opened unto us.

But then we find a question that I needed to consider in verse 9. The question asks, What kind of parent would give his child that he loves something they did not request? Of course we all would most likely respond with, "I would never do such a thing!" None of us would give our children anything that could harm or hurt them because we love them! And so it is with God. He loves us even more!

Verse 9 reveals a deeper truth, which is, if a son (child) should ask for bread, would we give that child a stone? Or if they ask for fish, would we give that child a serpent? The message here is that, what you and I may think is a stone could be bread! What we may believe is a serpent could really be a fish! I believe that what God is showing us here is that His provision may not always be in the form that we are familiar with; however, it will be provision just the same!

We can't be put off by what that provision may look like or how it may appear. We must do as the prophet did and just obey the instructions of God.

We must know and believe that He loves us! We must believe that God is in control of our very lives and that His love for us will not allow Him to abandon us. His love toward us is infinite and never changing, even when He instructs us to change. His love is constant and never changing!

As women of faith, it is vital that we understand how He loves us!

God's love is loyal. It is relentless and limitless. There are no boundaries to His love for us, and perfect love will cast out all fear, even the fear of change! There are many of us, especially women who have been cast down for many years. We have been made to feel as less than, not good enough, not pretty enough to the point that we hold ourselves in contempt! This saddens me greatly because there is so much value and worth inside every woman that God has created.

Every woman that has accepted Jesus as her Savior and Lord is filled with *His* spirit and full of *His* ability. We have been graced with *His* presence and contain valuable gifts, talents, and abilities. We have been commissioned to share the love of God in this world. However, because we operate from a platform of fear instead of faith, we hold back. We have been held back as well as held down. But today, through Jesus Christ, God has lifted us up to the realm where He placed us from the beginning! We are designed to be in positions of power and authority. It is God who has called us to be the head and not the tail! It is He who has set us above and not beneath.

We must remember that when God designed Eve by taking her out of the man, she was already equipped for Adam. Her purpose was already decided by God and was inside of her!

Once we begin to realize that truth, we will come to understand that our greatest fear is change. The fact is that change will affect every woman differently. Each of us will be unique, and there is no need or room to feel inadequate. It is not necessary to compete with another woman once we realize that our purpose and plan in this life has been given to us by God. As we make ourselves available to Him and open ourselves up to move as He instructs, each of us will become all that God intended for our lives!

Each of us will transform into that woman—that woman by God's design. She is unlike any other! She is not a carbon copy or duplicate of another sister! She doesn't need to mimic or make herself to appear as someone else. I have been noted as saying that no matter what part you have, how large or small, give it your all! If you are the eyelash on the body, though it seems insignificant, be the best eyelash that you can be! Why? Because that eyelash is vital. Although it may be the smallest, less noticeable, and looks like a fringe, it serves a great purpose. It is there to protect the eye from foreign substances, including dust and debris. Never underestimate your place in life! God's grace will always be sufficient, and we will always have adequate supply to meet every need.

My sister, you must take courage to believe God has called you out to be yourself and yet to represent Christ in every aspect of your life. As a woman by God's design, we are fearless and open to change. We know that as we obey Him, our lives will be blessed. The Lord, our God, has given us this promise: "You will experience all these blessings if you obey the Lord your God: Your towns and your fields will be blessed" (Deuteronomy 28:2–3).

I believe that when we are not open to change, we miss out on the total transformation of who we *really* are, and God's intent never reaches completion!

We must embrace the seasons of change in our lives, my sisters! Our needs will change. Our dreams will change. Our goals will change. Even our friendships will change. We are constantly transforming and becoming the complete woman by God's design, and that process will be in motion all the days of our lives.

CHAPTER 8

The Woman's Greatest Emotion—Love

As a young girl, it was my desire that one day I would fall in love, be married, and raise a family. I knew, at a very young age, that I wanted children, and I wanted a large family because I had plenty of love to share with a spouse and children. My husband and I married when we were quite young and began a family soon afterward.

For most of my married life, I only thought of love as a feeling or a good emotion. Most of the music that was played on the radio that had anything to do with love was always about how it would make you *feel*. Every recording artist had plenty to sing about the ups and downs of love. In fact, one artist weaned it down to a mere secondhand emotion.

Over time, as I read and studied the Word of God and received revelation, I came to realize that man's definition of love is mostly superficial, conditional, and very incomplete.

The truth is, although there is an emotional element to love, it is certainly much deeper and more powerful than just emotions and feelings. Our emotions come and go and can range anywhere between euphoria and depression on any given day. None of us feel perfectly *fine* all the time.

As I meditated in the Word of God, the Holy Spirit began to teach me about God's love toward me. It was at that point I understood that man's definition of love was the cheaper, not the deeper. Let us review the scriptures below that speak about love.

> Love is very patient and kind, never jealous or envious, never boastful or proud, never haughty or selfish or rude. Love does not demand its own way. It is not irritable or touchy. It does not hold grudges and will hardly even notice when others do it wrong. It is never glad about injustice but rejoices whenever truth wins out.
>
> Love never gives up, never loses faith, is always hopeful, and endures through every circumstance. (1 Cor. 13:4–7)

God's love toward us behaves in this way. His love remains consistently the same. His love is loyal, faithful, and constant.

I concluded that love is a *decision*! God decided to love us even when we were unlovable. He did not wait on us to demonstrate our love toward Him, instead He made the decision to demonstrate His love toward us first!

Once that decision was made, the behavior would follow.

We can define behavior as *the way in which one acts or conducts oneself, especially toward others. Additional descriptions of behavior are functioning, performance, action, and response.*

I have now come to realize, through my own life experiences as a wife, a mother, and a grandmother, what true love really is. True love only comes from the heart of God! It is operative in our lives only when we come to know God, for it is knowing Him that gives us revelation of who we are in Him! God Himself *is* love, and His love is the one and only true love because His love is not just natural, it is supernatural.

> And we have known and believed the
> love that God hath for us. God is love; and
> he that dwelleth in love dwelleth in God, and
> God in him. (1 John 4:16)

No man or woman can truly love until *their heart* has been touched with the love of God, and their mind has been renewed with the Word of God.

The love of God in a woman's life is totally sacrificial. Because love is the very nature and essence of God, it does not permit you to be selfish. For as the scripture says, it does not demand its own way!

To truly demonstrate the love of God in our lives requires a decision to do so—yes, a decision! Love is not an automatic feeling that we shut off and on at will. Instead it is a decision that we make daily. It is not limited to or dependent upon how I feel on any given day. Instead, it is supported by my decision to yield myself to the leading of the Holy Spirit and walk in love. I understand now that love is not a reflex. Let me explain further. When you and I have a reflex, that suggests that we are reacting to some type of stimuli, an involuntary, unplanned action that is done in response to something or someone.

Love, on the other hand, is not involuntary; rather it is voluntary, acting of one's own free will. This is God's love toward us. He, of His own free will, decided to love us even when we were not positioned to love Him in return. That is real love. This kind of love does not wait; it initiates! This love does not require; rather it inspires! That is the love of God! His love is genuine because it is of His own free will. A woman by God's design understands that she loves freely and without hesitation. Her love is authentic and genuine, not veiled. It is not hidden or masked for any reason; it is completely expressed openly, without boundaries or restraints. It is love in its purest, untarnished, and refined state. This is the love of God that has been shed abroad in our hearts by the Holy Spirit.

That doesn't mean that you have no rights or that you should be taken for granted, but it will mean that you consider the other person and prefer them above yourself. Most of us wouldn't dare to love this way on our own. It will take the love of God to give you the desire to love the way that He loves. This love can hold out and hold up well because it is made to last forever. It is not fleeting or inconsistent; it will endure. This love can't be demonstrated, relying on yourself only. It will require your dependence on God! Why? Because God is love, and His love is supernatural.

To love as God intended is an act of the will. It prompts you to make the decision to love, although it may not be reciprocated. It motivates you to love others because you love God first and desire to please Him. Your desire to please God overrides your natural and personal desires, which is the reason God's love is so powerful.

As I began to meditate on 1 Corinthians 13, the mysteries of love began to unfold for me. Once I made the decision to believe it, receive it, and do it, it became easier. I would no longer wait for an emotion or feeling only, but I would exercise my faith and become more loving, more accepting, and more forgiving! When you meditate on these verses, you will see the person of Jesus! It speaks of love as being able to endure. Love is kind. Love is not jealous or envious. It is not self-seeking. It is not rude. All of this is a perfect description of Jesus, our Savior, who willingly loved us so much that He gave His life in order that we may have life. He didn't seek His own way but lived to please the Father!

This is a loving behavior, love in action!

My eyes were opened to really understand what love was and is for the first time in my life. As I began to apply this revelation in my marriage, the Holy Spirit was now free to strengthen me, counsel me, and assist me in walking in this love.

As I looked back over the early years of my marriage, I thought about how young my husband and I were when we joined in marriage.

As I remembered the early years of our marriage and the progression of our lives together, I must confess that it was God's love *for us* and *in us*, which was the supernatural force that has held us together. God's love is the power train that keeps us encouraged to get up each day and remain together, depending upon the love of the Father working in both of us.

As a woman by God's design, I must realize that God's love is a sacrificial offering that is given freely to us every day of our lives. And in turn, we give it to our spouse, our children, our grandchildren, our colleagues and coworkers, and everyone that we care about. Everything about love, the genuine love that the scripture teaches, is always about others. It is never about just you yourself. Once I came to realize this, I was set free to love.

I decided within my heart that I would be like Jesus and love completely.

We, women by God's design, must learn to *will* ourselves to love. Just do it. Why? Because God Himself is love. He just loves us freely and without restraint.

Oh, how He loves us! He has no motive or agenda for loving us; He just loves us. His love for us is genuine!

I have learned to purposefully love not because I feel it, but because I have decided to do so! The world cannot understand this kind of love because it is supernatural. Jesus is the manifested Word of God in flesh, and God is love! First John 4:7–8 reminds us that we should love one another because everyone that loves is born of God and loves God. We are identified as followers of Christ because of the love that we show toward one another.

> Dear friends, let us continue to love one another, for love comes from God. Anyone who loves is a child of God and knows God. But anyone who does not love does not know God, for God is love.

Another witness is in Romans 5:8.

> But God showed his great love for us by sending Christ to die for us while we were still sinners.

We see here again that it was God who demonstrated His love toward us *first* even when we were not lovable, He loved us. Even when we were alienated from Him, He loved us!

There is *no* substitute for love. You can find salt substitutes, you can find sugar substitutes, you can even hire a teacher substitute for a class, but you will never find a substitute for *love*! Love must be genuine, authentic, and sincere.

Just as God is real, His love in us must be real! It is not loaded with fillers and anything artificial.

In *John 3:16*, it states, "For God loved the world so much that He gave his only Son, so that anyone who believes in him will not perish but have eternal life."

The scripture clearly shows us here that not only did God love us dearly, but he also *behaved in such a way to* show and manifest that love toward us by giving his *only* Son, His best gift.

God put His love into *action*. God was the one who started the love relationship because He loved us first. He extended the first love.

Love is the supernatural divine power that God used to change the very course of mankind! When God sent *Jesus*, He sent His love.

According to Hebrews 1:3, Jesus is the brightness of God's glory and the express image of His person. Jesus is *love*.

Nothing can stand against the power of love. Nothing can separate us from God's love. In Romans 8:35–37, This question is raised or asked:

> Can anything ever separate us from Christ's love? Does it mean he no longer loves us if we have trouble or calamity, or are per-secuted, or hungry, or destitute, or in danger, or threatened with death, no, not! Despite

all these things, overwhelming victory is ours
through Christ who loved us!

Remember this, my sisters, God is love! And He has already decided to love us, choose us, and anoint us to walk in love.

I encourage you to keep on loving each other with the love of the Father.

And finally, my dear sisters, let us, who live in the light of God's word, walk in love toward all people, be clearheaded, and know that you are protected by the armor of faith *and* love. Continue to encourage each other and build each other up as you have always done.

And now, may the God of peace and God of love make you holy in every way, and may your whole spirit and soul and body be kept blameless until our Lord Jesus Christ comes again. Let us rise and walk in love!

CHAPTER 9

The Woman's Greatest Setback— the Little Girl Inside

I realize that many of the women reading this may not have had the best childhood experience. Unfortunately, none of us had anything to do with the family that we were born into. We were not able to select our mother or father; we were just born into this world as a result of two individuals coming together and making sexual contact.

There are many of us who have never met our biological father or our sperm donor, for he was not in our lives in any form or fashion. Perhaps you never knew who your seed provider was, and you didn't have a "stand in the gap" father, so there could be a void in your emotional makeup because of this. Perhaps your soul cried out when you were a baby or a teenage girl, and even now it still cries out, although you are a full-grown woman. Many times, we don't even realize how incomplete and empty that emotional component of our soul is until many years later. You see, God intuitively gave each of us an emotional gauge that begins working on day one and continues to operate throughout our lives.

This same infant girl continues to grow, mature, and soon she is developed enough to distinguish positive emotion versus negative emotion. She begins to understand which emotion she prefers and does not necessarily appreciate anyone who brings anything else. Yes, her emotions are embedded in her soul. Her emotions began to develop when she was born. Even as a newborn baby, when she cried, she expected someone to come and comfort her. If she never received the comfort that she desired, she would now learn the emotion of abandonment and rejection.

Many of these same women are scarred today as adults and hurt because there is a little girl in them that is crying out. She wants to be heard and understood. She is the same little girl that may have been abandoned, rejected, sexually molested, seduced, and even deceived as a young woman. It is a fact that every experience in our childhood leaves a footprint on our lives that can never be erased.

So what happens to the baby girl that may not have had the two-parent home or even the child who may *have had* a two-parent home but one parent was usually absent—yes, physically in the home but emotionally absent!—or even the baby girl raised by a single parent, a parent that worked night and day in order to make a living and take care of the children in the home, a parent that never deposited anything of value or worth into the little girl's emotional wellness?

She may not have ever been told that she was loved by her father. She may have not ever been hugged or even held by her father. And even though she didn't realize or even understand it at the time, it would eventually render her emotionally deprived! Oh yes, because God created mothers and fathers to help children experience *His love!* Perhaps she didn't get that wholesome, complete, unconditional love, and therefore her perspective on wholesomeness is very warped.

She may have been abandoned early in life or even rejected. Perhaps her emotional growth was stunted because when she cried, no one came to check on her, at least not right away and sometimes not at all. When she vocalized what she wanted to say, no one thought it was important enough to listen to her. Perhaps this baby girl grew up in an environment where she didn't really feel loved but was more tolerated instead of celebrated. All of us have emotional scar tissue in our souls!

Scar tissue is a marking on the skin where it healed *after* an injury or trauma. Oftentimes, after an injury, scar tissue will form on its own and act as a protective barrier to close the gaps between the damaged skin and the injury itself.

This is also very true as it may apply to our lives. You see, when we, as women, have been hurt, abused, rejected, abandoned, and the list goes on, we can develop emotional scar tissue! Oh yes, when asked how we are, we confidently respond with "I am fine!" We say that we are fine, and we are well.

However, when you look down inside of us, when you locate that past injury or traumatic episode that we experienced, now you have discovered the scar tissue! You have now seen the barrier that was formed by us to protect us from opening our hearts and being vulnerable in that place. Yes, we confess that we are healed, and yet that place where the scar tissue is remains a very sensitive place, and we won't allow anyone in that place ever again! Yes, we move on with our lives, and we did survive the injury, but we need an escape from that emotional scar tissue. Many women today wrestle with these fears daily. We live under a veil, a covering that serves as a barrier between the real person of who we are and the real world in which we live. Under this covering, we feel protected and safe, and yet it is a disguise! We have bottled up so much of ourselves, and we present only the portions of who we are in pieces and never allow anyone to see us as exactly who we are.

How will this impact the young woman that she is becoming? I believe it will leave a big void in her emotional growth.

I believe she will struggle with feeling good enough. And as a result, she will spend a great deal of her adult life living to please—yes, please—anyone in any way in order to be appreciated and to feel whole.

She will always try hard to perform so that she can get the prize at the end of her performance and will never really understand why she never received it after all her efforts. She will be the baby girl that grew up into young adulthood with very little self-confidence and self-worth. But she won't dare to ask for anything from another person because she knows and remembers that when she cried, no one came, not right away, and oftentimes not at all.

Soon she will reach young adulthood and still may not realize that there has always been an emotional void in her life, so now she understands and knows how to hold her feelings back for fear of being abandoned and rejected.

Now she has been self-taught to not trust anyone or become vulnerable with anyone, especially in an emotional way. Oh yes, she has learned how to show everyone what she wants them to see and not her true self. Oh, how sad for her! She is emotionally scarred.

This young woman does not want to trust anyone because she doesn't want them to get her before she can get them. She doesn't want anyone to know or to see all the scars in her soul. She yearns for some emotional care. She just wants to connect with another human being. She has no real desire for anything like marriage or a covenant-based relationship; she will just only trust herself with another human being for a small, brief segment of their time because she feels so unworthy to even allow herself to dream of a lasting relationship. No one would want her, so she thinks.

Let us review the scripture in John 4:5–18, where Jesus met the woman at the well.

> Eventually he came to the Samaritan
> village of Sychar, near the field that Jacob

gave to his son Joseph. Jacob's well was there; and Jesus, tired from the long walk, sat wearily beside the well about noontime. Soon a Samaritan woman came to draw water, and Jesus said to her, "Please give me a drink." He was alone at the time because his disciples had gone into the village to buy some food.

The woman was surprised, for Jews refuse to have anything to do with Samaritans. She said to Jesus, "You are a Jew, and I am a Samaritan woman. Why are you asking me for a drink?"

Jesus replied, "If you only knew the gift God has for you and who you are speaking to, you would ask me, and I would give you living water." "But sir, you don't have a rope or a bucket," she said, "and this well is very deep. Where would you get this living water? And besides, do you think you're greater than our ancestor Jacob, who gave us this well? How can you offer better water than he and his sons and his animals enjoyed?"

Jesus replied, "Anyone who drinks this water will soon become thirsty again. But those who drink the water I give will never be thirsty again. It becomes a fresh, bubbling spring within them, giving them eternal life."

"Please, sir," the woman said, "give me this water! Then I'll never be thirsty again, and I won't have to come here to get water." "Go and get your husband," Jesus told her. "I don't have a husband," the woman replied.

Jesus said, "You're right! You don't have a husband— for you have had five husbands, and you aren't even married to the man you're living with now. You certainly spoke the truth!"

I find it interesting that this woman was going about her daily routine, busy doing her chores. I should mention also that she most likely drew water from this well daily, yet she herself was thirsty. Oh yes, this woman was very thirsty. Her thirst was not for the physical water that was in the well, but she was thirsty for spiritual water that would quench her very soul. On this day, her routine was interrupted by Jesus. Isn't it amazing how we can be moving about doing our usual activity, and then suddenly we are interrupted? Most of us don't welcome interruptions because they cause us to pause or stop what we are doing and yield ourselves to another matter. In most cases, we try to avoid as many interruptions as we can. However, on this day, there would be a divine interruption for this woman, and it would be one that she would not be able to avoid. On this day, she would experience an interruption that would not only cause her to pause, but it would change her entire life path! This day would bring sight to her blinded eyes, and she would begin to see what she had not seen before.

During her dialogue with Jesus, He instructed her to go and get her husband and bring him out. The woman's response was, "I have no husband." And upon hearing this, Jesus commended her for her honesty and replied, "You have well spoken and said the truth, for you have had five husbands, and the man you are now living with is not your husband."

Upon my initial reading of these scriptures, I thought perhaps Jesus was being very direct and even a little abrupt with this woman. However, as I continued to meditate on the passage, I began to understand why He was speaking with such bluntness. He had recognized the pain and the rejection that this woman was dealing with even more that she herself did. He did not want to waste another moment of her life; He wanted to save her! It is like when you call 911 for assistance; you can't afford to waste any time getting that person the help that they need. There is no time for a lot of meaningless babbling. They need help, and they need it now! This woman needed immediate attention. She, like so many of us, had been searching for the counterpart of her emotional makeup. She, like most women, just wanted someone in her life to complement and bring her some happiness. She also was aware that Jesus talking with her seemed quite unusual because the custom of the day was that Jews did not have dealings with Samaritans. So perhaps she viewed herself as less than, not worthy enough, and even not good enough. She was a woman who had accepted the low-ranking position of life. But this day would be differ-ent! She had been looking for someone who could touch and complete her soul. Every husband that she had was unable to fill that void in her life, so her quest was always to replace each of them as they moved out of her life. Imagine how desperate she must have been to constantly yearn and long for the emo-tional gap to be filled in her life. Even after five marriages, this poor woman found herself still in need of another person in her life to bring her fulfillment. I believe this was the reason Jesus wasted no time during their conversation when He instructed her, "Go get your husband." He already knew her situation, but He did this to show her that even after five marriages, and now a live-in companion, you are still alone! You are still unfulfilled! It is quite apparent that this woman was searching for that special person, the one and only, whom she had hoped would bring her total satisfaction. Even this woman had shifted somewhat from her usual pattern, yearning for that connection that she so desperately needed. She had already had five husbands, but this time, she had even settled for a man who was not her husband.

She, in her desperation, had settled to just live with some-one this time, since marriages had not given her what she had hoped to receive.

This helps us to see clearly the cycles of how her life had been. Many of us have probably been caught up in cycles and not even realize it. It is an ongoing, never-ending pattern that keeps pulling you back even when you know you need to move forward. It keeps you in a state of regular rotations with the same patterns and movements. Your life never really changes completely but only in part with a different face of a new partner with a distinct personality. She would turn again and again to this same cycle because she believed it would bring her satisfaction.

She needed to be validated in some way, and she only knew how to do this by marrying and remarrying repeatedly.

What pattern do you find yourself repeating? What is it that you continue to recycle over and over in your life simply because you believe this time it will be better? Why do we continue to do the same thing repeatedly and believe that the results will be different?

In her case, it was a marriage cycle. However, for many of us, it could be something else. This longing to be loved, accepted, and validated could present itself in another fashion. For some, it could be a constant turnover of transitions and movement from one person to another. You settle down with a person. You give your body, your emotions, all that you believe you should give, only to come to that point where it ends, and then you start again. You never find contentment with anyone. For others, it could be moving from one geographical location to another, and yet never finding contentment with any place. For others, it may be a never-ending cycle of substance abuse, such as alcohol, drugs, and other stimulants. You start and stop and yet never find peace and serenity with anything.

All these things give you a sense of completion but only for a season. And when that season comes to an end, you find yourself back at the start-up place, needing a repeat performance when you know it will soon end again. You may be a woman who never feels satisfied with anything. Your continual thirst is never quenched. Your appetite for life is never satisfied. You spend much of your money by constantly purchasing every new outfit in the hope that you can convince yourself that you are beautiful! You overindulge yourself with beauty products and shop until you drop madness, but even that does not reach the deepest pit in your soul or quench your ravenous thirst! No matter how much you achieve and how long you perform, it all seems like a long, winding cycle that has no end, leaving you exhausted, frustrated, and feeling incomplete.

But Jesus was not there to ridicule or to shame her! No, that was not His plan. Jesus had not come to condemn this woman, neither does He condemn us. In John 3:17, it states, "For God did not send His son into the world to condemn the world, but to save the world through Him." His plan was to show her God's love, the highest form of love! He was there to bring refreshment to her parched and thirsty soul! He was there to lift her up, not to put her down.

As you continue to meditate on the dialogue between this woman and Jesus, you soon realize that it was Jesus who offered her "living water." Consider this: This woman had drawn phys-ical water from this well day in and day out.

However, she never even realized that it was not this water that she really thirsted for; she thirsted for spiritual water. It is quite remarkable when we consider the benefits of natural water that our bodies need each day. Water always quenches our thirst completely, although many times we fail to drink water. We reach for all sorts of beverages—coffee, sweet tea, fruit juice, sodas—and we drink more of those than we really should, only to deprive our bodies of the pure water that it craves! And the irony of it all is that our physical bodies are mostly made of water! From a spiritual perspective, that should tell us something. The part of us that was created in the image of God is spiritual. Our spiritual being is constantly craving for refreshment, the refreshment of the living water, and His name is Jesus! We may fill our lives with many things in this life, but nothing or no one can replace what we truly need and desire, and that is Jesus!

She, like many of us, needed to make a connection with Jesus. And on this day, she did! The moment that she decided to accept the water that Jesus was offering, that was the day that all her emotional thirst ended! Yes, this was the day the woman was healed and set free from her emotional baggage! She realized that something had changed. Jesus had awakened her in her mind, her will, and her emotions! This woman had been trapped in a cycle for years and doing only what she knew to do, which was to reach out to another person over and over, hoping to be made whole and complete. But nothing and no one could satisfy her completely. They could not touch that place inside of her that really needed the touch of Jesus! Jesus was the only one that could understand her suffering, see her emotional scar tissue, and really love her the way she needed to be loved!

No matter what our past negative experiences were, in Christ Jesus, all has become new! Jesus had no hidden agenda. He only wanted to offer this woman a gift, one that she had never been offered. He wanted to bring deliverance and healing to her sin-sick soul. He wanted to bring restoration, revival, and refreshment to this woman! You see, my sister, we are incomplete without *Jesus*! He alone is the only one that understands us completely and still loves us!

In the book of Proverbs, chapter 14, verse 12, it states, "There is a way which seems right unto a man, but the end thereof are the ways of death." This is what this woman had done. Perhaps she had hoped that each marriage would bring her happiness, but they had not. She had thought that each time would be better, but it had not. The only thing that she had received was an unfulfilled life with endless cycles! I am reminded of another scripture in Isaiah 55:8–9 that says, "My ways are not your ways, and my thoughts are not your thoughts, for *my* ways are higher than yours, and my thoughts are higher." On this day, this woman became acquainted with God's way, which was Jesus! He is the way, the truth, and the life.

He is the only one that can bring about a real change in our lives. He is the living water! He is the life giver. He desires to return us unto Himself so that He can heal us and make us whole.

He understands our past hurt, rejection, abandonment, failures, weaknesses, emotional depravity, and yet He offers us living water with the promise that if we drink of Him, we shall never thirst again. His love toward us is pure, sincere, genuine, and refined.

This is a glorious revelation when we realize that in Him, we all have a new beginning, a new start, a new page to rewrite our life, our future! "Therefore, if any man be in Christ, he is a new creation; old things have passed away; behold, all things have become new" (2 Corinthians 5:17)! We can step into a freedom that we have never experienced before. All the old things are now passed away, and we are now new in Him! Is anyone thirsty? Come and drink, even if you have no money! The Lord Jesus is waiting with open arms to receive you just as you are.

CHAPTER 10

The Woman's Greatest Asset—Her Faith

As I consider a woman in the Bible whose life parallels most closely to mine, I would have to choose Sarah. We remember Sarah as the wife of Abraham. Her husband, Abraham, was considered as the patriarch of faith because He believed God, and his faith was credited to him as righteousness.

> And Abram believed the LORD, and the LORD counted him as righteous because of his faith. (Gen. 15:6)

Sarah had to be a woman of faith herself to be married to a man like Abraham. God promised him that He would give the land to Abraham's descendants. At the time when the promise was made, Abraham and Sarah had no children, but he believed what God had spoken. At that time, Abraham was seventy-five years old.

> So, Abram departed as the LORD had instructed, and Lot went with him. Abram was seventy-five years old when he left Haran… Then the LORD appeared to Abram and said, "I will give this land to your descendants." And Abram built an altar there and dedicated it to the LORD, who had appeared to him. (Gen. 12:4, 7)

Now let's fast-forward almost twenty-five years later, and the Lord appeared to Abraham again, confirming the promise that He had made years prior!

> When Abram was ninety-nine years old, the LORD appeared to him and said, "I am El-Shaddai, God Almighty.' Serve me faithfully and live a blameless life. I will make a covenant with you, by which I will guarantee to give you countless descendants." (Gen. 17:1–2)

God is still speaking of Abraham's descendants, yet Abraham and Sarah have yet to conceive and birth a child. When God appeared to Abraham at this time, he was now ninety-nine years old, and his wife, Sarah, was now ninety!

As we continue to read, we learn that three men came to see Abraham on a particular day. One of the men brought up the subject again that Sarah would bear a son. And when Sarah heard that conversation, she laughed! Although Sarah has been viewed by many in a negative way because of her reaction to this conversation, I was inclined to take a closer look at her. I wanted to place myself in her position in that moment and try to understand the human heart.

Many have accused her of not having faith in God; however, I would like to explore some other reasons. I don't believe she doubted the ability of God. I think, in that moment, she laughed because of the limited ability of herself!

She knew that her physical body had aged greatly, and her husband, Abraham, was even older than she was! In that moment, her mind considered the many years that had now passed, and she recalled the pleasures that she once enjoyed when they both were young, vibrant, and full of life. I believe, Sarah laughed because it was just easier to laugh than to cry. Have you ever had a moment in your life when if the truth were told, you would have just broken down in tears, but instead, you chuckled on the inside? You managed to laugh just so that you could move past the hurt that you were really feeling in that moment! In that moment, Sarah had a quick flashback of all the years she had wanted a child, and that child had yet to be born! She might have come to the resolve that she needed to move on with life and be thankful for what she *did* have and not focus so much on what she *did not*. Think about her position for a moment.

What happens to a woman when God's timing seems questionable? How should you feel when it seems that His lack of intervention is hurtful, and His promises are doubtful? You have been expecting to see the manifestation of His Word come to pass in your life, and yet there is nothing. What should you do when you have been disappointed countless times and disillusioned, and yet you are still standing, hoping against hope? Perhaps Sarah had learned how to process her unmet desires and beliefs in another way. Maybe she had made the decision that life wasn't so bad after all, and she had settled down inside her soul and just tried to live through all the pain and disappointment. Could it have been that at this point, even her marriage had been strained since she had offered her handmaiden, Hagar, to her husband Abraham for him to father a child since she had not been able to do so? Imagine her shame and disappointment when after so many years of waiting to conceive, she was still labeled as a barren woman! I believe, Sarah was trying to cope with all these memories in those brief moments, and then her only response that she could offer was to laugh—yes, just laugh.

When a woman has been waiting for a long time without fully understanding why, she will learn to cope in a different way. Let us examine this further for a moment. As women, we were designed to conceive, incubate, and to give birth. We understand the trimesters of a pregnancy. Each segment of time has a start and an end as the unborn child continues to develop.

We go through this whole process, which takes nine months. At the end of those nine months, we deliver. We now have successfully fulfilled that season, and we are now ready to move on to our next season.

Women are seasonal beings. We are designed to function in cycles and rhythms. We contain a built-in rotation of movement and timing within us. This is how our Creator designed us! If for any reason those cycles are interrupted or absent, we know within ourselves that there is something out of sync. Think about this: Our physical bodies were designed to repeat the same cycle every twenty-three, twenty-five, or twenty-eight days. This cycle happens every month, usually around the same time of the month. If that cycle functions as it should, we usually feel okay with it. However, if it does not, that is our signal that our bodies need to be checked by a medical professional. This is who we are and how God designed us as women. Overall, I believe we are our best selves if the natural and spiritual cycles in our lives start and end as they should.

We then are like beautiful chords of music being played on an instrument. Each chord is played with a certain rhythm and timing. There is also a melody to accompany each note so that when it all works together in harmony, it is a tapestry of melodic sounds, which echo the sound of music. If there is anything off, even by a little, it creates discord. If the timing and rhythm are not in place, and the melody is compromised, we now hear it as noise!

We have a built-in window of time that we can comfortably wait, but then when we exceed the wait time, we may become somewhat anxious. Waiting may be a little more difficult for us than for our male counterparts because, again, we are creatures of cycles. Let us be reminded that waiting is challenging for us. We don't want to wait for endless hours for anything that does not give us a clearly defined end goal. I believe, as women, we function best when there is a begin time and an end time. Let us consider this scripture:

> Gen 8:22 While the earth remains, seed-time and harvest, and cold and heat, and summer and winter, and day and night shall not cease.

As women, I know that we understand, in life, there will be seasons for waiting, and we're okay with that; however, we may struggle with the *length of waiting* required, especially when there seems to be no end to the ongoing cycle.

You must understand that a woman can wait, and we will wait. But once we have exceeded that wait time and gone way beyond, we may become disconnected and uninterested.

A woman who is constantly waiting will grow weary, and she will grow tired! She is ready to move on to the next beginning of something new, something different, and there are times that could be harmful!

Yes, I can relate to Sarah. I am certain, in that moment, she reflected on all the women around her, specifically her handmaidens that had borne children right in her presence. And yet here she was, the wife of a faithful patriarch, such as Abraham, and she herself was barren! Consider the years of waiting and believing that the promises of God would come to pass in her life.

I can identify with how she must have felt. Sarah probably had helped women around her in their time of giving birth and becoming mothers, and yet she herself had never experienced what God had promised her and her husband.

Imagine if you will the faith she must have had to rise every day for twenty-five years and live through the days, weeks, and months continually passing by. It took faith for this woman to maintain her dignity during the day when all eyes looked upon her, probably in hope that today would be the day Sarah would make the announcement, but she did not. I can only imagine the silence of the night seasons. It was then that Sarah probably faced her greatest challenge to hold fast to what God had said. It was in the quiet, still of the night when Sarah, now in the tent, prayed to God to bring the promise to past, as He had said, only to awaken early the following morning and repeat another day of the same thing.

Day by day she served Abraham. Day by day she took care of all the responsibilities as she had done before, yet without any evidence that God would make good on His promise. Have you ever waited on the Lord for something? Have you ever trusted Him with all your heart and yet the timing of the promise seems to be delayed? Do you know what it is like to hold on for years, believing the promise of God to come to fruition in your own life as you continue to stand with countless others in faith and prayer and witness their promises coming to fruition?

Yes, Sarah had gone through all of this, not because she wanted to or because she asked for this plight but because she was the wife of Abraham. She was committed to her husband through the good as well as the bad. She was not a perfect woman and had made some unwise choices, but the one thing that she continued to demonstrate was her faith. She showed her faith in God, even when her understanding of His plan was limited. She continued to remain in place, standing by the side of her husband, Abraham. Sarah knew how to stand! Through all the disappointments, she remained in place. Though she was mocked by Abraham's mistress, she remained faithful. She remained loyal through all the years. This is what faith will do. It will give you the strength to remain and to endure hardship, like a good soldier. It will create within you the ability to face each day, although yesterday did not produce what you expected. It will teach you to look up when you have many reasons not to. Somewhere deep inside of this woman and in many of us reading this right now, there is faith. Though it is small as a mustard seed, it is great faith. It takes faith to wait on the Lord and to be of good courage! It takes faith to be of good cheer when you feel that your life has been placed on hold. It takes faith to continue to walk in love toward the "Hagar" in your life when she despises you! It takes faith to stand day by day and to keep believing that the promise of God will come to pass in your life, although life is passing by. Oh, Sarah, I salute you! You waited. You stayed the course! You stood with your man, your husband, in faith, a woman that received the ability to conceive a child even when she was long past the normal age for it because she considered Him who had given her the promise to be reliable and true to His Word!

> By faith Abraham, when he was called to go out into a place which he should after receive for an inheritance, obeyed; and he went out, not knowing whither he went. By faith he sojourned in the land of promise, as in a strange country, dwelling in tabernacles with Isaac and Jacob, the heirs with him of the same promise: For he looked for a city which hath foundations, whose builder and maker is God.
>
> Through faith also Sara herself received strength to conceive seed and was delivered of a child when she was past age, because she judged him faithful who had promised. (Heb. 11:8–12)

CHAPTER 11

The Woman's Greatest Advantage—Prayer

I recall, as a young Christian woman, one of the first things you are taught to do in Sunday school is to pray! If you were involved in your local church in any capacity, the word *prayer* is not foreign to you. Everyone would make mention of it from time to time because prayer is essential. Although this is true that prayer is vital in the life of a believer, I personally believe that it must be approached with the right posture of one's heart. In other words, it should not be seen as ceremonial or as a religious ritual. I believe wholeheartedly that it should be passionate, heartfelt, and powerful in order to be effective. The book of James, chapter 5, verse 16 teaches us this principle.

> Confess your faults one to another, and
> pray one for another, that ye may be healed.

The effectual fervent prayer of a righteous man availeth much.

We are qualified as righteous upon the acceptance of Jesus Christ as our personal Savior and Lord.

I believe as a woman one of the greatest advantages for us is the gift of prayer. What a powerful spiritual tool we have as women of God! I am reminded of a woman in scripture by the name of Hannah. She had a situation in her life that was completely changed when she prayed.

There was a certain man of Ramathaim Zophim, of the mountains of Ephraim, and *his name was Elkanah* the son of Jeroham, the son of Elihu, the son of Tohu, the son of Zuph, an Ephraimite. And he had two wives: the name of one was Hannah, and the name of the other Peninnah. Peninnah had children, but Hannah had no children. This man went up from his city yearly to worship and sacrifice to the LORD of hosts in Shiloh.

Also, the two sons of Eli, Hophni and Phinehas, the priests of the LORD, were there. And whenever the time came for Elkanah to make an offering, he would give portions to Peninnah his wife and to all her sons and daughters.

But to Hannah he would give a double portion, for he loved Hannah, although the LORD had closed her womb. And her rival also provoked her severely, to make her miserable, because the LORD had closed her womb. So it was, year by year, when she went up to the house of the LORD, that she provoked her; therefore, she wept and did not eat. (1 Sam. 1:1–7)

It was not unusual in their culture for a man to have multiple wives, so this was not a strange practice to Hannah.

It was also a Hebrew man's posterity in having a son to perpetuate his name. And although having a child was a desire for Hannah, the Lord had not blessed her womb to conceive a child. However, regardless of the culture or the custom, it would be difficult for anyone, especially a woman, to feel disrespected and humiliated in her own home!

Each year, her husband would make this trip to worship the Lord. Elkanah prepared the yearly sacrifice and shared portions of it with both his wives in accordance with his custom.

We see that although Hannah had no children, Elkanah would give her a *double portion,* which was more than her share, because of his love for her.

When his other wife Peninnah learned of this, she began to sneer and make hurtful comments to Hannah. Hannah was feeling badly about the comments, and she was so hurt. It is one thing to be hurt by people on the outside—strangers, random folk—but when you are hurt by people on the inside, people that you care for and supposedly care for you, that is another level of pain that runs very deep.

Hannah finds herself feeling humiliated by the treatment that Peninnah was showing toward her. But then something changed for Hannah. You see, a woman can love tirelessly for a very long time, even decades. But when that woman is tired of being mistreated, she is fed up with all of it and decides today is not the day. Everyone in her path may need to leave the room.

Because of our unique makeup, we can hold and incubate whatever is inside, whether it is good or whether it is not good. We will and we can contain it until we can't.

This was the day that Hannah decided, no more. I will not allow this woman to continue treating me this way. I will no longer tolerate this behavior from her.

I have taken all that I can and all that I plan to take in this life from this woman. This is it. No more!

In that moment, Hannah was provoked! She was pushed beyond her capacity of feeling any limitations, boundaries, or restrictions. When a person has been provoked, it tells us that they are annoyed and very angry. They have been stimulated with a strong unwelcomed reaction. Every woman can identify with this realm because it is not like anything else you have ever felt or experienced. This is the realm where you will explode with all your feelings, all your emotions, and every part of your soul!

You will empty out everything that you may have been carrying inside. It is a breaking point. Because once the emotional container bursts, all the contents of your very soul will be emptied. Every year, it had been the same for Hannah. She had been silent with no reaction and held that all inside. She had gone along and held her peace in order to get along. Each year, these emotions had been building up, yet she suppressed them. But now, she had grown weary after being taunted, laughed at, and scoffed at by her rival wife, Peninnah, year after year!

It had been so painful for Hannah that all she would do was cry so much that she couldn't even eat! But this time, it would be different. This trip would be like no other.

It is important to note that Hannah did not retaliate against Peninnah. Although it was Peninnah who triggered the bottled-up emotion that had now been tapped into, she did not counterattack Peninnah. Hannah instead took a higher level. She elevated her prayer! She raised her prayer to another level. She boosted it to a higher position of importance. Hannah already knew the Lord. Hannah loved God, and she believed that He would help her. She believed that God would show mercy toward her, so she poured out of her soul unto the Almighty! She made this prayer more impressive and stirring. When Hannah went to the temple this time to offer a sacrifice, she would also make a special covenant with God. Her heart was so full, and she was crying and fervently praying to God.

And she made this vow: "O Lord of Heaven's Armies, if you will look upon my sorrow and answer my prayer and give me a son, then I will give him back to you.

He will be yours for his entire lifetime, and as a sign that he has been dedicated to the LORD, his hair will never be cut." (1 Sam. 1:11)

Hannah had now come to realize something that she may have never considered. She discovered her strength when she prayed. It was then that she realized she had the advantage! Yes, this prayer would be the one that would give her the breakthrough.

I believe that as Hannah prayed, her heart could feel what she may have not realized before.

She had stood strong in these trying times in her life, and she had remained standing through the tests of time. She had stood despite the storms of life, and yet it seems that nothing really changed. But today would be Hannah's breakthrough. Today she would reach heaven with her heartfelt prayer, and heaven would respond!

Hannah was praying so passionately that Eli the priest thought she had been drinking! He noticed that her mouth was moving, but he did not hear what she was saying. Sometimes in life, we may find ourselves in this situation. We may find ourselves in a meeting boardroom, a classroom, a laundry room, a hospital room, even a bathroom, and we may need to pray. Our physical location does not matter. We can pray fervently and still not disturb anyone around us. We may not be able to give voice to our words, but thank God, we can still pray, and God will honor the position of our hearts. It is wonderful when we finally receive a revelation from the Holy Spirit. It is like our eyes now see what we may have overlooked before. Often we may have neglected to pray because we see it more as a duty instead of a privilege. As we begin to realize that prayer is direct communication between us and God, we will have more of a desire to pray. It is a time when we can cast all our cares upon Him, knowing that He cares for us. Prayer is also a two-way time of fellowship because we not only talk to God, but we also listen to Him as He speaks to us.

When we consider how much God loves and cares for us, we should always hasten to talk to Him in prayer. Many times we limit ourselves because we fail to pray. We sometimes think that we have the answers, the solutions, the ability to solve the problem, but we must remember that we are limited! We can only reach a certain point, but God is unlimited. He is all-knowing, all-powerful, and He has no boundaries. Hannah tapped into this dimension when she prayed. This was the day that she not only prayed but also made a covenant with God! She requested a male child from the Lord, and her prayer was specific. She didn't pray in generalities with vague phrases, she was precise in her request. Not only was her request specific, but her vow unto God was also. She promised God that she would give this son back to Him for His service all the days of his life.

Hannah made a commitment to God because she was a woman of faith.

Often, we, as women, forfeit so many blessings in our lives simply because we fail to pray. We fail to tap into that realm where God is and to have that dialogue with Him. We may have forgotten that without Him, we can do nothing. It is in Him that we live, we move, and have our being! He is our source of all that we need. Every resource that we have comes from Him, our Creator.

We must remember that in Him is life. We must never forget that we now have the privilege of talking to God whenever we want to do so. When we call upon Him, He hears us. And because we know that He hears us, we believe that we have those petitions and desires of our heart.

Now that you and I have been made righteous because of the shed blood of Jesus, we can begin to pray even more. Prayer allows us to get closer to our Heavenly Father. Prayer also reduces anxiety and gives us a sense of calm. It also teaches us how to be grateful and give thanks for all that God has given to us. Prayer will also help us to overcome the fears and temptations that we are faced with in this life. And finally, prayer positions us for miracles. Prayer causes us to triumph in every situation. It places us in the best position because we have communicated and contacted God. This, my sister, gives us the advantage!

CHAPTER 12

The Woman's Greatest Victory—the Perfect Finish

Each of us will face challenges every day; however, the joy comes in knowing that God is with us. He has always been with us, and every trial and test that we faced enabled us to learn valuable lessons. Every step that we make as a woman by God's design is purposeful! We have learned also that every situation that we may have encountered did not disrupt the plan of our Creator.

It is such a blessing when we, as women, understand all that our Creator has given to us through Jesus, and every goal that we desire to achieve can be achieved. The work that God the Father has begun in us, He will finish. We know that God is with us, working His good pleasure on the inside of us, and He will complete that work. Philippians 2:13 says, "for it is God which worketh in you both to will and to do of his good pleasure."

Every season in our lives has served a purpose, and God continues to mature and develop us in Him as we experience these seasons. I know there have been times in our lives when we may have asked the question, "Why doesn't God take away hardships and crises?" But all those episodes are designed to bring maturity in us! Psalm 138:8 says, "The LORD will work out his plans for my life. For your faithful love, O LORD, endures forever. Don't abandon me, for you made me." I have come to understand that God is always with us. He has not promised us that our lives would always be a smooth ride. Instead He has promised us that He would be with us on the ride. He promised us that when we passed through the fire, we would not be burned. And when we walked through the waters, we would not be drowned because He is with us. We are not exempt from the tests and the trials, but we are assured that God is with us.

It is a fact that God designed each of us with a specific plan to be fulfilled in our lives, and we are here for a specific purpose. As we become more aware of His presence with us and His spirit inside of us, we then come to realize His plan at work in our lives. As we begin to understand that we were created with a purpose, we will then understand that every creation of God has a life assignment! Every aspect of our lives is the result of the choices that we decided to make. Even when those choices were not to our advantage, God was able to make those work together for our good when we trusted Him. He will not allow anything to exist without purpose and fulfillment.

God will not allow anything to go to waste, for He is a purposeful being in all that He does.

> You are worthy, O Lord our God, to receive glory and honor and power, for you created all things, and they exist because you created what you pleased. (Rev. 4:11)

Every woman by God's design will come to this realization in her life. Although we were deceived by the serpent at the beginning of creation, God's plan remained intact. He had already declared a blessing upon our lives! His plan had already been sealed over us, and there was nothing that would change that. My sisters, when the Word of God goes out, it will always accomplish that which God wants, and it will never return unto Him void! That same Word will prosper in the thing where it was sent!

> The rain and snow come down from the heavens and stay on the ground to water the earth. They cause the grain to grow, producing seed for the farmer and bread for the hungry. It is the same with my word I send it out, and it always produces fruit. It will accomplish all I want it to, and it will prosper everywhere I send it. (Isa. 55:10–11)

When we believe what God has declared about us, we will follow His instructions with care and with precision because we clearly see that our purpose is hidden in following His instructions. We will no longer be afraid of changes and transitions that may come in our lives because we understand that God's purpose is being carried out on our behalf.

We can also come to a mature place in our lives and realize that it is not how we started in this life but how we will finish! We will no longer hold hurt and malice in our hearts for what others have done to us. We will leave it all in the past and reach forward into our future. None of us were responsible for the beginning of our lives, but all of us must take responsibility for how we live our lives! Therefore, it is vital that during our lifetime, we come to know Jesus as our personal Savior and Lord. He is the only one that can bridge us back to the Father, our Creator. Once we have been bought back to that place in God, our vision now changes. Our vantage point takes on a new perspective! Now we see life through Him, and we become more understanding of our place and purpose on this planet. We begin to appreciate those around us, who God has placed in our lives. We recognize those who were sent by God to help us mature and deposit goodness into our lives. By the same token, we will begin to recognize those who have not been sent by God and bring nothing to enhance our God-given purpose. In Christ Jesus, we come to understand that our past doesn't matter. For in Him, all things become new. We are now a new creation created in Him! Where we came from or how we got here becomes less significant, for we now have set our eyes on Jesus.

We now realize that He is the author and the finisher of our faith! I am reminded of a scripture found in John 6:11–12.

> Then Jesus took the loaves, gave thanks to God, and distributed them to the people. Afterward he did the same with the fish. And they all ate as much as they wanted. After everyone was full, Jesus told his disciples, "Now gather the leftovers, so that nothing is wasted."

I share this scripture above because I believe it will further illustrate my next point.

Jesus was going about with His earthly ministry during this time. It had been a full day, and a multitude of people had been with Him all day because they had seen His miracles. In this same chapter of John, we read in verse 5 that Jesus realized that there was a great multitude of people around Him, and he asked one of His disciples if they needed to buy bread (food) for these people to eat. We see the human side of Jesus. He was aware that the people were now hungry, and they needed to be fed. We see His human compassion. Another disciple informed Jesus that the only thing that he had seen among the crowd was a young boy who had two small fish and five barley loaves. As you continue to read, we see that Jesus instructed His disciples to have the people sit down.

After everyone had been seated, Jesus then took the loaves, along with the fish, and offered a prayer of thanksgiving to the Father and distributed the food. What happened next was a miracle. Now we see the divine side of Jesus. The fish and the bread began to multiply. There had only been two fish, but now there would be hundreds more. The bread had been limited to only five loaves, but now it would be unlimited. The bread and the fish would now become a bakery and a fish market. The supply had been stretched and expanded to reach the masses! Why? Because Jesus had given thanks to God for what He *did* have, and God had blessed it. God had placed favor upon it! God had multiplied it several times over to the point that there were baskets left! This is the awesome power of God, who is El-Shaddai, the God who is more than enough! The people had eaten all that they wanted and had been completely satisfied. No one needed anything further, for they were filled to the full. The purpose of the loaves and fish had been completed. But there is still something more that I wanted to really understand. Upon continuing to meditate, I began to get a deeper and clearer revelation. Verse 12 says that Jesus instructed the disciples to gather up all the fragments that remain, that *nothing* be lost! What? You mean Jesus, the Son of God, was now collecting fragments? Why would He have any interest in fragments? In fact, why would anyone have a need for fragments?

It is here that I began to see the heart of God. My sisters, fragments are broken pieces and portions that have been separated from something whole. They are bits and remnants of something greater.

Once they are separated, they are no longer a part of that which is whole; however, their composition still consists of that which is whole.

In other words, when you break off a piece of fruit and share it with someone, the piece that was broken off, though it is not whole, still has the exact same composition of the whole. It still has the nature of the whole and the constituents of the whole, although it is not the whole itself. It may not be as filling as the whole piece of fruit, but it is still functional. After meditating on this truth further, I realized that Jesus could not leave the fragmented pieces tossed on the ground to be trampled on by the feet of men! He needed to collect them. He wanted to pick them up and save them! Why? Because those fragments represent all of mankind! Yes! Those fragments represent broken, torn, scattered, and separated pieces of each of us. We were separated from the Creator, our Heavenly Father, in the beginning because of one man's disobedience. His name was Adam. But now, today, we are bought back into wholeness with our Heavenly Father because of one man's obedience! His name is Jesus. For as by one man's disobedience (Adam) many were made sinners, so by the obedience of one (Jesus) shall many be made righteous (Romans 5:19).

It is Jesus who picked us up, saw the worth and value in us, and decided that "nothing would be lost." To Him we were worth saving! It was Jesus who came to the earth for this purpose and this purpose only: to save those who were broken, torn, and separated from the Creator. He did not come to demonstrate or display His royalty, but He made himself of no reputation and took upon him the form of a servant and was made in the likeness of men (verse 8). And being found in fashion as a man, he humbled himself and became obedient unto death, even the death of the cross (Philippians 2:7–8). He came to save all of mankind! He knew and understood that though we were torn from our Creator, we still had been created by Him! We had already been blessed to multiply and replenish the earth. We had already been given the authority to reign in life from the beginning. God will never withhold anything that He has promised to us. He knew and understood that our Heavenly Father had already blessed us in the beginning. Because of this, Jesus knew that once that blessing had been spoken and decreed over our lives by God, it would surely come to fruition. So He instructed His disciples to gather all the fragments that had fallen off because all those pieces were still of value! It doesn't matter what we have done, we are still God's creation! It doesn't matter how we may look right now; Jesus still loves us! It doesn't matter how ugly we may think our lives may appear; Jesus still sees us as beautiful creations of God. We can trust Him. He will not abandon us. He will never leave us nor forsake us! Therefore, He came, He lived, was crucified, and resurrected from the dead. He did all of this to prove that He was the Son of God and the only one who could offer mankind the salvation package! His body was broken so that we could be whole! We no longer should accept our fragmented lives! We can trust Him to bring us into complete wholeness. I pray that there is someone reading this today who will trust Jesus as your Savior. I pray that you will allow Him to come into your heart. He really loves you so much!

All you need to do is receive Him by faith, right now, and allow Him to do the rest. "If you openly declare that Jesus is Lord and believe in your heart that God raised him from the dead, you will be saved. For it is by believing in your heart that you are made right with God, and it is by openly declaring your faith that you are saved" (Romans 10:9–10). He sees your end from the beginning! He alone is our champion, and He will be there to assist us in achieving the purpose of God in our lives. His shed blood has redeemed us from sin, death, and hell.

We are now positioned back in our rightful place with the Heavenly Father. We now have been justified and declared righteous. When God, our Creator and our Heavenly Father, sees us, He now sees the cleansing blood of Jesus, and that blood has washed away all our sins. We are now friends of God, and we have peace with Him. We can be reinstated to our rightful position that God intended from the beginning. We were created in His image and His likeness. We are second to no one! We are a woman by God's design!

About the Author

Cynthia McGill is a native of Durham, North Carolina. She is a wife, mother of three children, and grandmother of five. She enjoys traveling, and on occasion riding as a passenger with her husband on his motorcycle. She also enjoys reading, writing, and listening to music. Her life of ministry spans more than four decades wherein she has served in several capacities, ranging from minister of music to copastor alongside her husband. Cynthia enjoys meditating and teaching the Word of God, providing spiritual counsel, and being a source of encouragement to others. Her greatest joy is motivating, mentoring, and observing the spiritual growth and maturity in other Christian women as they apply the principles of scripture in their spiritual, professional, and everyday lives.